THE LIBRARY OF
AMERICAN
LIVES AND TIMES™

JOHN SUTTER

Sutter's Fort and the California Gold Rush

Iris Engstrand
and Ken Owens

PowerPlus Books™
New York

Published in 2004 by The Rosen Publishing Group, Inc.
29 East 21st Street, New York, NY 10010

First Edition

*Editor's Note: All quotations have been reproduced as they appeared in
the letters and diaries from which they were borrowed. No correction was
made to the inconsistent spelling that was common in that time period.*

Library of Congress Cataloging-in-Publication Data

Engstrand, Iris Wilson.
John Sutter : Sutter's Fort and the California Gold Rush / Iris
Engstrand and Kenneth N. Owens.
   p. cm. — (The library of American lives and times)
Summary: A biography of the man associated with the gold rush in
California, detailing his various business ventures and pioneering
exploits in California.
Includes bibliographical references (p.) and index.
ISBN 0-8239-6630-5
1. Sutter, John Augustus, 1803–1880—Juvenile literature. 2.
Pioneers—California—Biography—Juvenile literature. 3. California—
Gold discoveries—Juvenile literature. 4. California—History—
1846–1850—Juvenile literature. 5. Sutter's Fort (Sacramento,
Calif.)—Juvenile literature. 6. Sacramento (Calif.)—Buildings, structures, etc.—Juvenile literature. [1. Sutter, John Augustus, 1803–1880.
2. Pioneers. 3. California—History—To 1846. 4. California—History—
1846–1850.] I. Owens, Kenneth N. II. Title. III. Series.
F865.S93 E54 2004
979.4'04'092—dc21

                                    2002011978

Manufactured in the United States of America

CONTENTS

1. The Man and the Myth

John Sutter, California's best-known frontier adventurer and promoter, achieved spectacular fame because of one unforgettable incident: the discovery that set in motion the California gold rush. On January 24, 1848, in a ditch being dug to carry water for a new sawmill, Sutter's business partner, James Marshall, found flakes of gold, that rare and precious yellow metallic element known for its beauty and value worldwide. The site was on the American River, in the foothills of the Sierra Nevada, about 35 miles (56.3 km) northeast of Sutter's Fort, the commercial center of Sutter's New Helvetia colony. In the months that followed, thousands made their fortunes in the California gold rush, but John Sutter was virtually destroyed. The discovery of gold made him famous, but its consequences doomed his grand ambitions and caused his shaky business empire to crumble. Modern California sprang up around him, but John Sutter lost

Opposite: William Smith Jewett painted this oil portrait of frontiersman John Sutter around 1855. At that time, Sutter kept the title and the pomp of officer in the California militia, but he was deeply in debt and largely without influence in the new era of California politics.

everything through bad judgment, mishandling of funds, and a refusal to face his responsibilities.

This is the story of a complicated man. To many, he appeared to be a worldly, well-educated gentleman. He spoke German, French, English, and a little Spanish. He seemed kindly and caring to the immigrants who were settling northern California's wilderness. He gave them supplies, seed, and livestock so that they could begin a new life, and he hired many of them to work at Sutter's Fort. Yet Sutter pressed Native Americans into service, betrayed the Mexican officials who had given him land, and showed little consideration for his family in Switzerland. He failed to pay debts, cheated his partners, disrespected his marriage vows, drank to excess, and blamed others for his problems.

How did a man with so many faults become a well-respected citizen in a new country? For many admirers, his accomplishments overshadowed his failures. Circumstances often combine to make a hero of an ordinary man, and such might have been the case with John Sutter. Sutter schemed to make a hero of himself as well, and he built his colony and his hopes for fame on the personal myth he created for himself. An expert at self-promotion, Sutter's single-minded hope was to be California's most famous pioneer, and in this he succeeded. How he did so is a story of remarkable failures and defeats.

2. John Sutter's Early Life

John Sutter was born Johann August Suter on February 15, 1803, in Kandern. Kandern was a small town in the dukedom of Baden, just inside Germany's borders and 13 miles (21 km) north of Basel, Switzerland, the bustling center of Swiss trade. Johann's father, Johann Jakob Suter, worked as a foreman in a paper mill. His relatives were mostly small farmers from the Swiss village of Runenberg. Johann August's mother, Christina Wilhelmina Stober, was the daughter of a German clergyman from a small town on the Rhine River, an important waterway in western Europe.

Johann August's parents were not wealthy, but they encouraged in their son a love of books, an eloquence in speech, and an easy familiarity with influential people. Johann attended an elementary school in Kandern located near the bridge that French emperor Napoléon Bonaparte's armies used to cross the Rhine River on their way to conquer lands in Austria. During these years, soldiers were frequently stationed in the town of Kandern, and the sight of

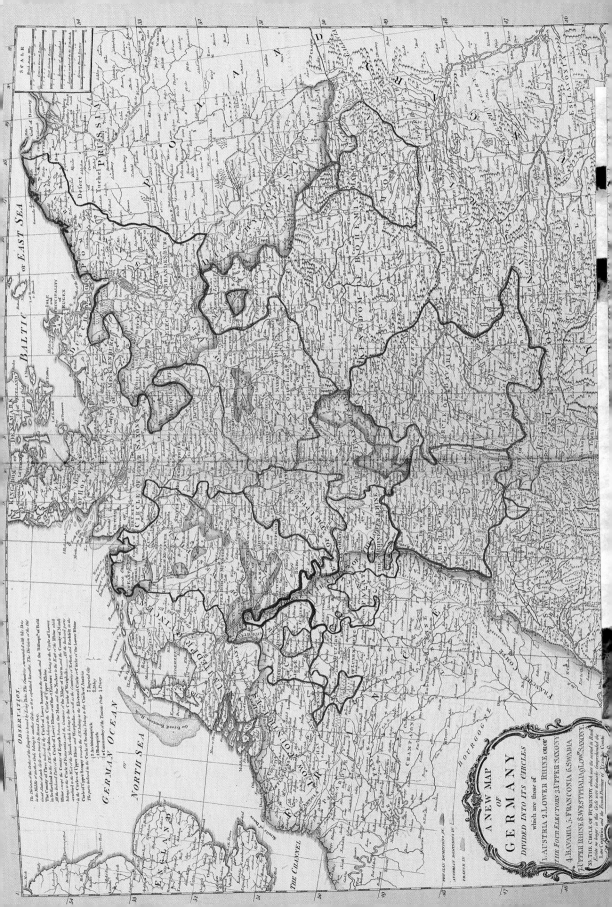

A NEW MAP
of
GERMANY
DIVIDED INTO ITS CIRCLES
which are those of
1. AUSTRIA 2. LOWER RHINE, OR OF
THE FOUR ELECTORS 3. UPPER SAXONY
4. BAVARIA, 5. FRANCONIA 6. SWABIA
7. UPPER RHINE 8. WESTPHALIA 9. LOWER SAXONY
NB. THE CIRCLE OF BURGUNDY which now is united to France
Exists no longer in this Circle are besides Comprehended the
Provinces and Principalities not known as the Imperial Counts

their brightly colored uniforms no doubt thrilled a boy approaching his teens.

Johann grew up with a romantic and fanciful view of warfare and military pageantry. He admired the French soldiers he saw, and he was especially impressed with Napoléon's strength, even though most European countries were united in an effort to defeat the French emperor. In January 1814, when Johann was ten years old, powerful European leaders, including the czar of Russia, the emperor of Austria, and the king of Prussia, met in Basel to begin a united campaign against Napoléon. The following year, Britain, with the support of these countries, defeated the French emperor and forced him to surrender his throne.

Three years later, fifteen-year-old Johann left his small German village to attend school in nearby Neuchâtel, Switzerland. After graduating, he moved to Basel to work as an apprentice for a publisher, bookseller, and printer. Basel offered many diversions to a young man, but Johann longed to return to the countryside. The only lasting effects of this apprenticeship seem to have been an appreciation of expensive books and an additional *t* in his last name, which he now spelled Sutter.

Johann, unhappy in Basel, left to become a clerk in a draper's shop, a fabric store specializing in draperies

---

Opposite: In the early nineteenth century, Germany was divided into many independent states, shown in this map, which were ruled by princes and local overlords. In 1805, Napoléon's army invaded, and the French occupied the country until 1813, when a coalition of European nations forced the emperor to retreat and later to give up his throne.

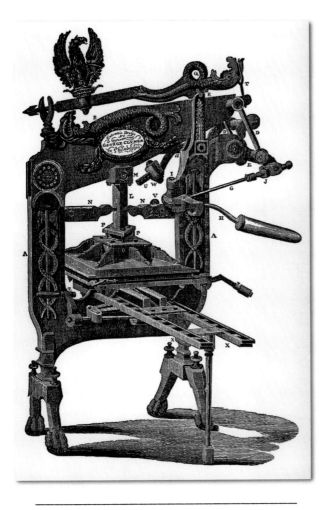

In 1813, George Clymer invented the Columbia printing press in Philadelphia, Pennsylvania. Soon the new machine, which was made of iron rather than wood, was widely popular in Europe. The diagram shown here dates from 1817. Johann Sutter would have worked with a press much like this one during his apprenticeship in Basel.

and curtains, in the small Swiss town of Aarburg. There Johann met a woman named Annette Dübeld, with whom he quickly fell in love. Johann quit his job with the draper, and he followed Annette, commonly called Anna, to her hometown of Burgdorf. He was no doubt pleased to find that Anna's widowed mother possessed considerable assets and lived comfortably, although she was not very wealthy. Johann took a job as a grocery clerk and continued to court Anna. Finally, on October 24, 1826, the couple married, and Johann Sutter received a large dowry from his mother-in-law of 2,000 francs. The couple's first child,

Johann August Sutter Jr., was born the next day. Four more children, Anna Eliza, Emil Viktor, Wilhelm Alphonse, and Carl Albert, followed. Carl Albert, born in 1833, died at age six.

Despite Johann's marriage to Anna and his residence in Burgdorf, he was, according to Swiss custom, considered a foreigner and therefore denied certain rights. Johann was at a disadvantage when competing for business with the merchants of Burgdorf. His mother-in-law gave him the money to open the Johann August Sutter & Co. dry goods store, where Sutter sold cloth, bedding, and sewing materials. However, the store was never a success. The people of Burgdorf, strictly bound by Switzerland's caste system, were suspicious of the outsider.

Sutter worked tirelessly to make a success of his dry goods business and even traveled the countryside to take orders for cloth, yarn, thread, needles, buttons, ribbons, and other related items from the farmers throughout the district. Nevertheless, he managed to run up more debt than profit. He tried to expand his business on borrowed money, but he fell deeper in debt. He took on an irresponsible business partner who soon stole Sutter's stock of goods and left him burdened with even more debts. In addition, Sutter consistently spent more money than he made. He always dressed stylishly, he bought expensive books, and he wanted luxuries he could not afford.

Always fascinated with the pomp of the military, Sutter joined a volunteer corps in Bern in 1828. An 1832 lithograph of Swiss artillerists illustrates the elegant uniform that Sutter would have worn.

In 1828, perhaps to escape the drudgery of his failing business and family life, Johann Sutter volunteered for a military reserve corps in Bern. He must have preferred soldiering to working in the store or staying home with a growing family, because he devoted much of his time and energy to the volunteer corps. Johann Sutter became a first under-lieutenant of the Second Center Company of the Third Battalion, but he never went to war.

By mid-May 1834, facing the threat of debtors' prison, Sutter sold all of his assets and made plans to leave Europe, most likely with Anna's assistance. He promised to send for the family later and headed for the port city of Le Havre, France. At Le Havre, he could board a ship bound for England and then the United States. He apparently had no plans ever to return to Switzerland.

On June 9, 1834, Sutter's creditors began bankruptcy proceedings against him, and the court issued a warrant for his arrest on June 12. The chief of police in Bern asked all police authorities in Switzerland to relieve Johann Sutter, if they intercepted him, of whatever money and valuables he might be carrying and to notify the Bern authorities of his whereabouts. Anna's mother died six months later, leaving Anna a small fortune of more than 25,000 francs. However, Anna could not claim the money. It was held by the authorities to insure the full payment of Sutter's debt, which totaled more than 50,000 francs. For years after Johann left for America, Anna remained virtually a charity case, living in poverty and disgrace while raising five young children by herself.

Even though Anna and her four remaining children would eventually be reunited with the adventurous Johann in America, the journey there was filled with hardship. Anna and her young family moved into her grandparents' home. She worked as much as possible, while her missing husband created a new life in the United States. Johann August Sutter, fugitive debtor and absentee husband and father, would soon reinvent himself as Captain John Sutter, a former officer in the Swiss army with important friends and rich business associates.

3. The Road to California

Johann Sutter landed in New York in July 1834, and with money given to him by Anna's family, he set out for the West in the company of two Germans and two Frenchmen. Most likely, Sutter had first learned of the West in the writings of Swiss traveler Gottfried Duden. Duden described the American West as a lush natural paradise. It was a place of opportunity for immigrant settlers and adventurers. Land and other natural resources were plentiful. The climate was varied, and the ground was fertile. Society was free of the rigid social structures of the East. Enterprising young men and women could find religious, political, and personal freedom in the West. It was the natural destination for a gambling man burdened by debt, kept down by a strict European caste system, and hungry for fame and fortune. Sutter traveled through Indiana to Ohio, where he parted company with his European companions. After staying in Ohio for a few months, he headed to St. Louis, Missouri, where a large community of German immigrants lived. At the Hotel Switzerland in St. Louis,

St. Louis, Missouri, long known as the Gateway to the West, rises from the banks of the Mississippi River just south of the mouth of the Missouri River. Since its founding, the city has been a crossroads for traders, settlers, and western explorers. George Catlin's painting, created around 1833, shows the city from the eastern bank of the Mississippi River.

Sutter met Johann August Laufkotter from Westphalia, a province in northwestern Germany. The two men, sharing a common language, got along well and stayed close friends for more than two years.

Taking a lesson from a chance meeting in St. Louis with a slick confidence man who claimed to be an ex-colonel in the service of Prussia, Sutter began to invent imaginary accounts of his own past. At thirty-one years old, Sutter was slim and handsome and had a military bearing. Though he had served as only a part-time

A party of traders gathers at Camp Comanche on the Santa Fe Trail.
They travel in ox-drawn freight wagons. These wagons could
carry great quantities of goods and were well designed for
traveling on uneven ground. Guarded by a small force of U.S.
soldiers, the wagons form a circle, which would provide
protection against American, Mexican, or Native American raiders.

infantry reservist in Burgdorf, he began introducing
himself as Captain John Sutter, an officer in the Royal
Swiss Guard. With his new identity, Sutter joined a
group of traders planning to go by wagon to the
Southwest along the Santa Fe Trail.

Already short of funds, Sutter sold some of his fancy
clothes in a St. Louis pawnshop and bought trade goods
with the money. He planned, with his friend Laufkotter
and several Frenchmen, to enter what was called the
Santa Fe trade between Missouri and modern-day New

Mexico, then still a part of the country of Mexico. When he reached Santa Fe, Sutter traded his goods for seven valuable mules and sold his small collection of trinkets to Santa Fe locals. Encouraged by his success, Sutter returned to Missouri. Back in St. Louis, Sutter sold the mules for a profit and treated his companions to drinks, but Laufkotter did not believe Sutter had shared his profits fairly. When Sutter planned another trade venture and his partners elected him captain, Laufkotter was critical of their loyalty. Sutter, he suggested, was not a man to be trusted.

During these years, most of Sutter's money appeared to come from legal trade, but some historians believe it came from various illegal or unethical business practices, too. Sutter undertook the trade of American goods for stolen Mexican mules and horses with the Apache Indians. Apparently caught participating in this illegal trade during his second trip to Santa Fe, Sutter saw a large part of his goods confiscated. The rest were sold for a fraction of the price that Sutter had paid for them. Sutter and Laufkotter were forced to work as clerks and cooks to survive in Santa Fe's depressed economy. Later they briefly tried mining for gold in old diggings in New Mexico and continued trading Mexican mules and horses in Missouri, but both ventures sent Sutter into debt. Laufkotter later accused Sutter of widespread underhanded trading and smuggling activities during his years on the Santa Fe Trail. Benjamin D. Wilson, a fur trader in New Mexico who later became mayor of Los Angeles, California, later accused Sutter of wrongdoings in the Santa Fe trade as well.

According to Wilson, Sutter had cheated some German merchants who had brought a few wagons full of trade goods to Santa Fe in 1836. Sutter offered to sell their goods for them. Sutter later reported that, after making the sale to some Mexicans downriver on the Rio Grande, illness had forced him to return to Santa Fe before collecting the money. One of the German merchants went downriver to collect the money from the Mexicans and found that not only had Sutter received payment in full, but also he had suddenly recovered his health and was on his way to Missouri with the profits. The Germans tried to catch Sutter and collect their money, but they were unable to overtake him. Eventually they let the matter drop. In Missouri, Sutter settled in Westport, or modern-day Kansas City, where he may have saved himself from bankruptcy by illegally selling whiskey to the Shawnee and Delaware Indians. After a failed attempt, in 1837, to build a hotel in Westport, Sutter decided to leave Missouri for California, also then a part of the country of Mexico. Rumor had it that the Mexican government was giving land grants to anyone who might settle in California, become a Mexican citizen, and attract other settlers.

The trip to California was no easy task in the 1830s. Settlers and adventurers could travel by wagon across the Great Plains, the Rocky Mountains, and the Sierra Nevada, or by schooner around the southern tip of South America. They could also go by ship to the Isthmus of Panama, cross the narrow strip of land, then take another ship up the western coast of Central America and California. All these routes were dangerous and expensive. Only the healthiest and luckiest adventurers could survive Indian attacks, fierce storms at sea, and tropical diseases. Sutter found safe overland passage with an American Fur Company expedition led by Captain Andrew Drips. The party included wagons and pack mules loaded with supplies for the company's annual trading rendezvous in the beaver-hunting region of the Rocky Mountains and was typical of those crossing the continent. It included travelers who went along for the safety provided by such a large party.

Among the travelers in 1838 were several missionaries and their wives, who were on their way to join the Protestant missions established by Marcus and Narcissa Whitman for the Indians of the Oregon Country. Also along on the trip were George Rogers Hancock Clark and William Preston Clark, sons of George Rogers Clark, a famous military hero in the American Revolution, and nephews of William Clark of the 1804–1806 Lewis and Clark expedition.

Driving rains, fatigue, the threat of Indian attacks, and other hardships made the trip extremely difficult.

The first fur-trade rendezvous took place on the Green River, in what is now Wyoming, in 1825. Fur trappers traded their furs for supplies, such as rifles, provided by the fur traders, who would then transport the furs east for sale in American and European markets. Alfred Jacob Miller painted this image of a caravan of trappers and traders in 1837.

The travelers hunted small game animals and killed an occasional buffalo, but food was always scarce. Following the North Platte River to present-day Wyoming, they passed by Fort Laramie and eventually arrived at the Green River site of the fur-trade rendezvous. At the rendezvous, the American mountain men and the Indians would trade their beaver furs for payment and supplies provided by the fur company's representatives.

Most of the trappers and traders, including Captain Drips, would not be continuing to the Pacific coast, so Sutter purchased a Native American boy from the traders. The Indian spoke some English and Spanish and could serve as a guide to Fort Hall, a trading post operated by the British Hudson's Bay Company in modern-day Idaho. From Fort Hall, the small party followed the Snake and Columbia Rivers, reaching the Whitmans' mission near Fort Walla Walla, in present-day Washington State, in mid-August 1838. Sutter was amazed when a few days later the Nez Percé wife of one of the hunters gave birth to a daughter at sunset after traveling 25 miles (40.2 km), collecting wood, making a fire, and preparing dinner for her husband. She proudly showed her newborn baby to the group the next morning.

When Sutter reached Fort Vancouver, situated on the north side of the Columbia River about 100 miles (161 km) from the Pacific Ocean, he had a letter of introduction to James Douglas, the chief trader at the Hudson's Bay Company fort. Sutter wanted to continue overland southward to California, but Douglas pointed out that crossing the Klamath Mountains with winter coming on would be difficult. Because there did not seem to be any other way to get to California directly, Sutter asked if he could book passage on the company's ship *Columbia*, which was sailing to the Hawaiian Islands, a kingdom independent from U.S. control at the time. In Honolulu, Sutter would look for a trading ship ready to sail for California.

Douglas agreed and charged Sutter £15 (15 pounds sterling), or about $75, for his cabin accommodations and £6, or about $30, each for Sutter's eight companions. In a report to the Hudson's Bay Company directors, Douglas stated that Sutter had served as a captain in the French army, had no connection with the United States, and had left Europe with a respectable fortune. Douglas's account echoes the fabulous story Sutter himself told. The report indicated that Sutter's present plans were to buy cattle in California and drive them to the Willamette valley in Oregon.

The *Columbia* sailed for Honolulu on November 11, 1838, and reached the harbor on December 9, just after the departure of a ship bound for California. The next ship going to California was not scheduled to leave until several months later. Sutter was forced to remain in Hawaii. Thanks to his versatility in languages and his charming ways, Sutter enjoyed the company of the well-established business community of the islands during his stay. He dined with the British and American government trade officials as well as with Faxon Dean Atherton, an upstanding Honolulu merchant who later moved to California. Within a short time, Sutter made the acquaintance of U.S. consul John Coffin Jones and William French, a leading Yankee merchant who maintained a monopoly on island products.

Sutter, with his polished manners, stories of amazing adventures, and exotic background, was quickly accepted into Honolulu society. He later claimed that the Hawaiian monarch Kamehameha III offered him command of the island's small army. When Sutter declined the offer, the king gave him ten Kanaka indentured servants, or native Hawaiian indentured servants, for three years. These two women and eight men would be the first "hired" laborers at Sutter's grand California colony.

Under Kamehameha III, the third king of a united Hawaii under the Kamehameha dynasty, Hawaii felt the influence of American and European exploration. On the advice of a New England clergyman, Hawaii adopted a constitution and a bill of rights. The king was photographed by Henry L. Chase between 1850 and 1870.

Throughout his stay in Hawaii, Sutter continued to tell stories about his supposed experiences as an officer in the Royal Swiss Guard in French service. His self-promotion was extremely successful. The French and Greenaway Company in Honolulu agreed to give him more than $3,000 in credit to outfit his California adventure. William French also agreed to hire a man named Captain John Blinn and to lease Blinn's ship, the *Clementine*, filling it with French's own goods for a trading voyage first to Russian-controlled Alaska and then to California. The ship would follow the roundabout ocean currents stretching northeast across the Pacific Ocean from Japan. Sutter went aboard the *Clementine* as French's unpaid supercargo, or business agent, a position that gained him a free trip to California.

When he finally sailed, Sutter took along flattering letters of introduction from Honolulu's leading merchants and officials. Accompanying him were the ten Kanakas, eight men and two women, who would settle with him in California. The eight men were experienced seamen and all were willing workers. Also on board were two German friends. As was John Sutter, these travelers were looking forward to a California adventure. In addition, Sutter took along a new pet, a fierce-looking bulldog, to guard the camp.

4. A New Beginning

With his small party, John Sutter sailed from Honolulu aboard the *Clementine* in April 1839. The ship's first destination was Sitka, the capital of Russian Alaska and the headquarters for the Russian-American Company. This private company directed Russia's Alaska colony, making profits by selling the skins of sea otters and fur seals in China. To supply their Russian workers with food, company officials had also established a small trading and farming outpost, Fort Ross, on the northern California coast, 60 miles (96.6 km) north of San Francisco Bay.

One of the first people to greet Sutter in Sitka was Captain Ivan Kupreianov, the commander in chief of all Russian territory in America. Aided by his charming wife, the former princess Menshikova, Captain Kupreianov entertained his visitor in royal style. No doubt Sutter retold the stories about his fictional military career. Certainly he was pleased to dress in his finest uniform, to sip French wine, and to dance the mazurka with the Russian princess until late at night.

Modern-day Sitka, Alaska, was founded in 1804, when Russian governor Aleksandr Baranov built the new headquarters of the Russian-American Company there. Baranov named the town Novoarkhangel'sk, or New Archangel. This photograph, which dates from around 1900, shows one of several blockhouses constructed to defend the Russian colony from the neighboring Tlingit Native Americans. The blockhouse no longer stands.

Speaking in French, the language of upper-class Russians at the time, Sutter and Captain Kupreianov discussed California. Quite possibly it was Kupreianov who first suggested that the lower Sacramento valley would be an ideal location for Sutter's settlement. The two men also talked about Fort Ross. Sutter must have been interested to learn that the Russians had not only farming equipment and large numbers of beef cattle, sheep, and horses but also cannons, muskets, and kegs of gunpowder at their Californian outpost. Sutter was gaining a new and more complete appreciation of the politics of northern California and the challenges he would face as a frontier settler.

After one month in Sitka, Sutter again boarded the *Clementine*, and Captain Blinn steered the ship southward toward California. Constant storms, with winds and high waves, made the trip along the Pacific coast long and dangerous.

At last, on July 1, 1839, the entrance to San Francisco Bay came into view through thick banks of fog. Carefully Captain Blinn guided his vessel past high cliffs, later known as the Golden Gate, and anchored just offshore from Yerba Buena. This small town, named "good herb" for the mint that grew along the shore, was the trading center for northern California. It housed an international community that included British, French, and American merchants and Mexican soldiers, along with Mexican Californian settlers and former sailors from a dozen nations.

A small boat soon brought Mexican officer Lieutenant Juan Prado Mesa to the *Clementine*. The ship could not remain in San Francisco Bay, the lieutenant stated, but must leave at once for Monterey, the capital of the province and the only legal port of entry in California. After Captain Blinn explained that he needed to make emergency repairs, Lieutenant Prado

The first European settlement at San Francisco was founded in 1776.
A party of 200 Spanish colonists, led by Captain Juan Bautista de Anza,
built a fort and a mission on the bay. By the time John Sutter arrived,
more than 60 years later, the town had grown into a thriving port.
This 1884 print shows the harbor as it appeared around 1846.

Mesa allowed the *Clementine* to remain in the Bay for
two days. When the ship was ready to sail, Sutter had
to turn down the invitation of Yerba Buena's American
merchants to stay and join in their Fourth of July cele-
bration. Instead, Sutter and the *Clementine* left port on
the morning of the Fourth, and the following day, July
5, 1839, John Sutter and his small company arrived
safely in Monterey harbor.

Sutter had been attracted to California by the
promise of thousands of acres (ha) of free land, offered

by the Mexican government to anyone who would promote frontier settlement. At a time when land was widely considered to be the most substantial form of wealth and the basis for status in society, this promise was almost too good to be true. On land granted by the Mexican government, Sutter intended to create a strong, prosperous colony on the northern California frontier, relying on hardworking immigrants from Switzerland and other European countries. During his travels, he had told everyone he met about his great project, gathering letters of introduction and promises of assistance.

When he met Governor Juan Bautista de Alvarado at Monterey, Sutter immediately impressed the governor with the letters he brought from U.S., British, and Russian officials. As one American at Monterey remarked, "No one has, ever before, come with so many letters." Governor Alvarado agreed to help the charming newcomer. First Sutter would need to locate the land that he wanted and begin building a settlement. According to Mexican law, Sutter could return to Monterey after one year of residence, take an oath of allegiance to the Mexican government, and be given legal title to the land by the governor.

By the time he met Governor Alvarado, Sutter had decided to build his colony somewhere on the lower Sacramento River. Though it lacked roads, this region could be reached by river navigation from San Francisco

In 1836, Juan Bautista de Alvarado led a small revolt against the ruling Mexican authorities and established Alta California as an independent state, appointing himself governor. In 1838, the Mexican government acknowledged his authority and officially appointed him military governor of California. Alvarado was a skilled politician, but his political career would not survive California's transition from Mexican province to U.S. territory.

Bay, and because Europeans, Americans, and Mexicans had not yet settled the area there would be no immediate legal threat to Sutter's claim. However, the area was still populated by Native Americans of many separate, small communities that were part of the Yokuts, Maidu, Miwok, and Nisenan cultural groups. A recent malaria epidemic had drastically reduced their numbers, but the Indians of the Sacramento valley were still considered a threat to white settlement by the Mexican Californians, known as Californios. The Indians sometimes raided the horse herds of large cattle ranches to the west, closer to San Francisco Bay. Controlling these "horse-thief Indians," as some officials called them, seemed impossible for the small, poorly armed Mexican military force.

In addition, Governor Alvarado, like other Californio leaders, worried about potential French, British, Russian, and American plans to take California from Mexico. He came to believe that this pleasant promoter, Captain Sutter, a talkative and energetic young man, could help to strengthen and defend Alvarado's province. Sutter convinced the governor that his colony would protect northern California from invasion by any other nation. He also promised to establish peace with the Indian peoples on this frontier, without the aid of Mexican soldiers.

With Alvarado's approval, Sutter sailed back to San Francisco Bay and began to prepare a colonizing expedition up the Sacramento River. At Yerba Buena, he

Malaria was first introduced to California in 1832 to 1833 by a Hudson's Bay Company fur-hunting brigade. No one then understood either the disease or its cause, or that infected individuals carried the malaria-causing microbes in their bloodstream. The disease could be transferred to others by mosquitoes, who passed on the infection with their bites. When infected members of the Hudson's Bay expedition reached the Sacramento River valley, where the air along rivers and streams was thick with mosquitoes, they set off California's first and worst malaria epidemic. The disease killed tens of thousands of Sacramento Valley Indians half a dozen years before Sutter's arrival, and it remained a deadly danger to everyone who entered the region.

leased the schooner *Isabel* from merchant Nathan Spear and loaded the ship with supplies, sold to him by Spear on credit. He also arranged to borrow two smaller boats, and he hired eight or nine unemployed sailors to accompany him and his Kanaka workers upriver. Sutter took along Spear's seventeen-year-old nephew, Hawaiian-born William "Kanaka Bill" Davis, as his guide on the voyage.

Early on the morning of August 9, 1839, Sutter gave orders for the *Isabel* and his two smaller boats to set sail. The trip was difficult. Young Davis got lost while trying to find a channel that led to the Sacramento River. The journey upriver turned into a tedious, slow voyage through the islands of the Sacramento delta. The boat struggled through a forest of tule reeds and vines and was surrounded by clouds of mosquitoes.

Heading upstream, Sutter's party was halted by a group of two hundred Indians, their bodies painted black, red, and yellow, who appeared suddenly alongside the river and made threatening gestures toward the *Isabel*. Telling his men to put away their guns, Sutter, unarmed, went ashore and began talking. "Adios amigos," he pronounced loudly with a German accent. Although his meaning, "Good-bye friends," was confusing, at least two of the Indians understood him and saw that this strange little group meant no harm. With gestures and a few more words of basic Spanish, Sutter explained that he had come to live in their homeland as

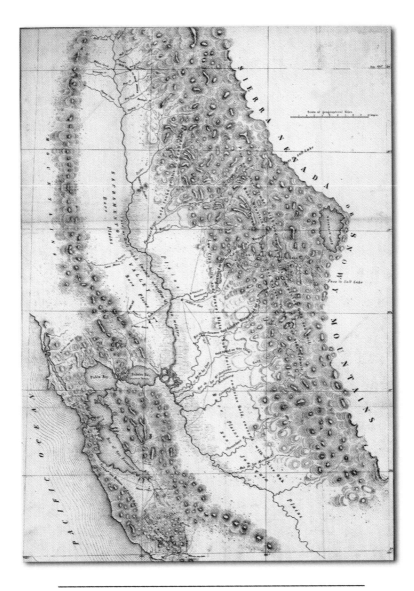

The Sacramento River is fed by the Pit, McCloud, Feather, and American Rivers, which are in turn fed by the rain and melting snow on the peaks of the Sierra Nevada. The Sacramento River is surrounded by some of the most fertile land in the world. As John Sutter approached the mouth of the Sacramento River in 1839, he was confronted with a thick maze of waterways, many of which had not yet been charted by Europeans.

a friend. If they would visit his camp, he let them know, he would make a treaty, or agreement of peace, and give gifts to them all.

An Indian who spoke some Spanish agreed to go with Sutter and show him the country upriver. With the aid of this man, Sutter first sailed past the mouth of the American River and scouted out the lower Feather River, where he would later locate his main farm. Then Sutter returned to the American River, took his boats a short distance upstream, and directed everyone to help unload the cargo on the south side of the river. On shore he set up his one cannon, preparing to defend the camp if necessary.

Standing in the middle of his camp that evening, surrounded by stacks of supplies and equipment he had bought on credit, with Indian visitors crowding about and staring at everything, John Sutter must have been pleased. He had reached the farthest frontier of California, and he was making a new beginning.

5. Ruling the California Frontier

The day after John Sutter landed, young Kanaka Bill Davis made ready to sail the *Isabel* back to San Francisco Bay. Staying at the American River camp with John Sutter were three white employees, ten Hawaiians, one Indian guide, and Sutter's bulldog. To mark the event, Sutter loaded his cannon and fired a salute. Nine times the cannon boomed. Years later Davis recalled the scene vividly. As the heavy blasts of the cannon died away, he wrote, the Indians were shocked and thrilled. Deer, elk, and other animals ran back and forth across the plains, at once startled and curious at the sound. The howls of wolves and coyotes rose up from the woods. Flocks of ducks and geese took to the air. Davis concluded,

Standing on the deck of the Isabel, I wit-
nessed this remarkable sight, which filled me

Opposite: Of his decision to settle in an isolated region rather than near the Californios of Sonoma, Sutter, shown here, said, "I noticed . . . that [among the Californios] the hat must come off before the military guard, the flagstaff, and the Church. And I preferred a country where I could keep mine on. In other words, where I should be absolute master."

with astonishment and admiration, and made an indelible impression on my mind. This salute was the first echo of civilization in the primitive wilderness so soon to become populated and developed into a great agricultural and commercial center.

What Davis described as a primitive wilderness was in fact already beginning to feel the effects of European and American frontier expansion. Spanish army officers and Franciscan missionaries had visited this country on tours of exploration and settlement, naming the Rio Sacramento, or River of the Holy Sacrament, and the Rio de las Plumas, or Feather River. American mountain men had been finding their way into northern California since Jedediah Smith led a trapping party across the Sierra Nevada range in 1826. British and French Canadian fur trappers working for the Hudson's Bay Company had first arrived in California from Fort Vancouver in 1832, beginning annual trips between the Oregon Country and the lower Sacramento valley.

Sutter did his best to make friends with his Indian neighbors. He was generous in giving gifts. The local Indian people liked cloth shirts and woven cotton blankets, called mantas in California, as well as bright beads, metal jewelry, and other articles for personal decoration. As a special favor, Sutter handed out small pieces of Hawaiian sugar, a scarce item. Sutter believed it necessary to demonstrate his military strength in addition to giving gifts. Occasionally he fired off his cannon and muskets, setting up targets and blowing them to pieces for Indian audiences. Without making any direct threats, Sutter let his neighbors know that he could protect his camp against any attack.

For Sutter and his workers, shelter was an immediate concern. Sutter erected a few simple tents, and the Kanakas built two Hawaiian-style grass houses. Before the winter rains began, everyone helped to make a supply of adobe bricks of sun-dried mud, with which Sutter's workers built a one-story structure, about 45 feet (14 km) long, that included storerooms, a kitchen, a blacksmith shop, and living spaces. For a roof, the Kanakas tied down tule reeds across wooden rafters. The simple building was Sutter's frontier-style headquarters until a more substantial fort took its place.

Sutter's bulldog helped to safeguard the camp. As Sutter sat up talking with a worker late one night, the two men heard a scream and a loud cry of "Oh Señor!" Rushing outside, they found a terrified Indian held tightly in the bulldog's jaws. They rescued the man and took him into Sutter's room, then heard another scream outside. The bulldog had a strong grip on a second equally terrified Indian, whom Sutter and his employee promptly rescued. While Sutter sewed up their wounds with silk thread, the two Indian men admitted that they were part of a raiding party that had meant to murder everyone in the camp, take over the settlement, and enrich themselves with the plunder. That night Sutter showed wisdom as well as bravery. He scolded the two men strongly, made them promise to behave well, then turned them loose without further injury or punishment as a gesture of goodwill.

Sutter routinely discovered Indians concealing weapons with plans to kill him, and he treated them firmly but peacefully, warning them that any future rebellion would be punished with death. Later challenges brought more aggressive responses, however. A neighboring Indian community, the Chacumnes, boldly resisted Sutter's control early in 1840. These people refused to work for Sutter and moved away from his settlement. Sutter refused to lose any part of his valuable workforce. He marched southward with a force of six whites to make a surprise attack on the Chacumne camp at night. Sutter's tiny command killed six Chacumne men without suffering any injuries. Though Sutter's behavior may appear cruel by modern standards, it was not uncommon at the time. When the surviving Chacumne leaders asked for mercy, Sutter told them that if they moved back to their old village and returned to work at Sutter's colony, he would forgive them. They did as he said, and soon a few Chacumnes became loyal soldiers in a small Indian army that Sutter created to protect his settlement.

Later that year, Sutter found it necessary to take harsher military action. A group of Indian strangers arrived at the fort. The strangers told Sutter that they were Christians from the Franciscan mission that had been located at San José. At their request, Sutter gave them permission to trade with the nearby Yalecumne settlement and even to buy wives if the Yalecumne women freely agreed to the bargain. The next day, Sutter learned from a frantic survivor that the visitors had attacked the Yalecumnes, had killed five of the men who tried to defend the community, and had kidnapped the women and children.

Sutter knew that such raids were common in California, carried out both by Indian bands and by lawless Mexican and American frontiersmen. He was determined not to have this happen in his territory. He armed twenty white men from his settlement and a greater number of Indian soldiers, marched after the raiders, and caught up with them 30 miles (48.3 km) away. What happened next is not known for certain, but the result was a victory for Sutter's men. He later stated that he had executed fourteen of the raiders by firing squad. When he wrote about the incident to a Mexican official, Sutter claimed he wanted "to show others an example; more, to [let them] see what bad actions get for recompense."

With money scarce in frontier California, everyone did business by bartering, or borrowing and paying back with trade items rather than with cash. Cattle hides were the most common form of currency in California. Sutter accepted cattle, horses, and sheep from Mexican and American ranchers, promising to pay later with wheat, cattle hides, or Indian-made woolen cloth and tools. He did the same with merchant Nathan Spear in Yerba Buena, who continued to send him supplies while never receiving full payment of his debts.

Using gifts and peaceful trade, threats, and harsh punishments, John Sutter succeeded in controlling and protecting the Indian peoples near his settlement. Until he left California, Sutter remained dependent on his Native American employees. He also continued to value his loyal Kanakas, all of whom decided to stay with him rather than return to Hawaii. One of the Kanaka women, Manuiki, had become Sutter's housekeeper and close friend.

By 1840, John Sutter's little settlement was well established. To pay his debts, Sutter raided the natural environment for products he could sell or trade. When salmon began their annual spawning run in the Sacramento and American Rivers, Sutter's workers netted thousands of the fish, put them in barrels with salt to prevent spoiling, and shipped them to merchant Nathan Spear at Yerba Buena. When the rivers flooded and stranded the region's elk and deer on small islands, Sutter and an Indian employee set out in a boat to kill these animals so he could send their hides to Spear as payment.

Sutter had less success trapping beaver. Despite costly efforts to make steel traps and to send out trappers, he could not compete with the Hudson's Bay Company fur brigades. Some of his own employees sold their furs to the British trappers, who offered higher prices. Even worse, Indians stole Sutter's traps to use the steel to make their own tools and weapons. Though surrounded by natural resources, Sutter often had difficulty providing for his growing colony and paying his debts.

The construction of Sutter's Fort was a major accomplishment. Because the whole area regularly flooded during the storm season, Sutter looked for the highest land near the American River. His site was more than 1 mile (1.6 km) south of the river, standing well above the flood plain. Here Sutter's Indian workers put up an adobe brick structure with outside walls 18 feet (5.5 m) high and 2 ½ feet (0.8 m) thick. Two towers rose above the walls on the northwest and the southeast corners, each with a cannon on its top floor to guard the fort's wide gateways. The walls enclosed an area 320 feet (97.5 m) long by 160 feet (48.8 m) wide, divided into workshops and living quarters surrounding a central courtyard. Sutter's main building was in the middle of the courtyard. Three stories high, it included storerooms, work space, Sutter's own apartment, and a small jail cell.

No other building in northern California at the time was half so magnificent as Sutter's Fort. Begun in 1840 and completed in 1844, it was constructed not just to protect Sutter's colony. It was a monument to his power and influence. As he was pleased to recall years later, Sutter held almost absolute power over

Sutter's Fort, shown here in a color print based on an 1847 engraving, was larger than the frontier settlements at Bent's Fort and Fort Laramie and was virtually impenetrable by cannon. The structure housed workshops, a bakery, a factory for making blankets, and a mill.

the Sacramento valley region in the early 1840s. "I was everything," he boasted, "patriarch, priest, father, and judge." Still Sutter's grand ambitions were not satisfied. He needed a fresh wave of immigrant settlers to join him and add their labor to the development of the colony he had named Nueva Helvetia, or New Switzerland.

6. The New Helvetia Colony

In August 1840, a year after arriving in California, John Sutter realized his hopes for a Mexican land grant. He returned to Monterey, took an oath of allegiance, and became a Mexican citizen. The following May, he presented Governor Alvarado with a petition for the lands that made up his colony, commonly called New Helvetia. The governor was pleased to give him eleven leagues of Sacramento valley land, or more than 75 square miles (194.2 sq km).

The New Helvetia grant included rich bottomlands in the flood plains along the lower Sacramento, Feather, and American Rivers, which extend eastward toward the foothills of the snow-capped Sierra Nevada range. The Sacramento River was the western boundary. The volcanic cones of the Tres Picos, known today as the Sutter Buttes, marked the northern boundary. The eastern boundary was very broadly defined as "the margins of Feather River," a description later interpreted as the eastern edge of both the Feather River and Sacramento River flood plains. The southern boundary was fixed by an

The New Helvetia grant, part of which is shown here with Tres Picos in the distance, covered some of the world's most fertile land. John Sutter and his ambitions for a great agricultural colony had significant consequences on the environment. Sutter and his settlers introduced new kinds of animals, plants, and diseases. They hunted elk and deer in great numbers, cut down dense stands of oak and cottonwood, and grazed their cattle in the fields of native grasses.

east-west survey line that touched the Sacramento River a few miles (km) south of the mouth of the American River. The grant included not only the area around Sutter's Fort but also a piece of property Sutter named Hock Farm, northward on the Feather River. The future city of Sacramento was within the grant's boundaries, as was the future site of Sutterville, a town downstream from Sacramento that Sutter would survey and promote just before the California gold rush. It was a lordly

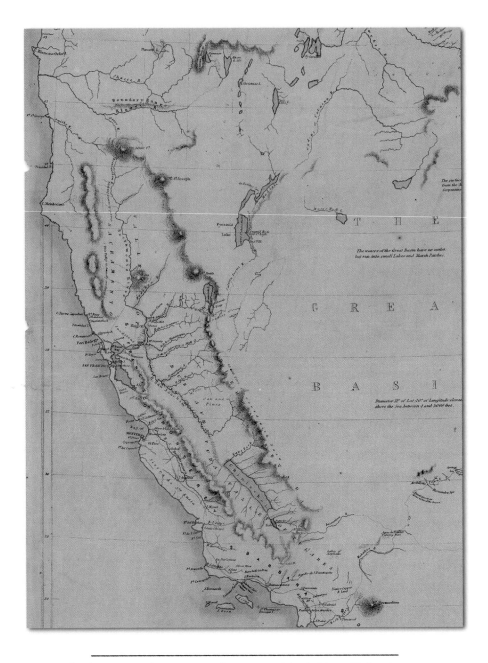

The location of Sutter's colony was ideal. New Helvetia was a frontier outpost, a port city, and a gateway to places farther east. As such, it attracted settlers traveling west, fur trappers and traders from as far north as the Oregon Country, and explorers preparing to cross the Sierra Nevada.

domain for a man who only six years earlier had fled Switzerland to escape his debts.

Sutter's New Helvetia grant came with conditions imposed by the Mexican government. He needed to establish at least twelve families of new settlers on his lands. He had to help defend California's borders against the enemies of Mexico. Governor Alvarado, following the Mexican government's common policy, directed Sutter to look after the region's Indian peoples, to protect their freedom, and to guide them in adopting the ways of the Euro-Americans, using only kind measures and gentle training. Sutter could not make war on the Indians, the governor stated, without first obtaining permission from the Mexican government. In addition to land, Sutter received an official appointment as "chief of justice and representative of the government on the frontiers of the Sacramento River," a title that he proudly signed to his documents thereafter.

Sutter told Governor Alvarado that the necessary immigrant settlers were already living at New Helvetia, but this was not entirely true. A few American and British men, most married to Indian or Californian Hispanic women, had come to Sutter's settlement, where he hired them as woodcutters, craftsmen, carpenters, and trappers. He encouraged these men to settle permanently on his land, but he needed to attract others.

In September 1841, Sutter discussed his plans in detail with a French visitor, who was greatly

impressed. "No branch of business is overlooked by this pioneer," the Frenchman wrote. When new colonists arrived, claimed Sutter, they would help him to grow wheat and vegetable crops for export. Sutter would raise dairy cattle to produce butter and cheese for market. In addition, Sutter declared, he would grow rice, cotton, and indigo in the valley, and grapes, olives, and fruit trees on the hillsides. In a few years, Sutter promised, New Helvetia would become a thriving commercial center. Trading expeditions would arrive there from Canada, the Oregon Country, and the eastern

United States. It was a wonderful dream, a vision of the future, and eventually most of it came true, but not under John Sutter's management.

Nevertheless, Sutter took a step toward achieving his goal that September. He purchased from the Russian-American Company everything at Fort Ross and the surrounding farms except the land, which the Mexican government claimed. The Russians were ready to abandon Fort Ross because the Hudson's Bay Company farms in the Oregon Country provided a more reliable, cheaper source of wheat and beef for Russian Alaska.

The terms of the sale were generous. Sutter agreed to pay $30,000 for the property over a period of four years. The first three payments were to be in farm produce, mainly wheat, delivered at Yerba Buena. The fourth payment, of $10,000, due in September 1845, was to be in gold coin. To guarantee the deal, Sutter gave the Russians the right to take over his New Helvetia property if he failed to make the payments.

The purchase of Fort Ross was a great achievement and a great risk. Immediately Sutter sent herders to drive the Russian colony's horses, cattle, and sheep over the difficult trails to New Helvetia. His employees began to take apart some of the buildings at Fort Ross and send them by ship to Sutter's Fort. They made other shipments of farm equipment and tools as well as the guns, the cannons, and the Russian soldiers' uniforms. Sutter had bought everything that he might need in the way of animals and equipment for his dream colony. He lacked only skilled, hardworking, reliable workers. Unless Sutter found laborers, New Helvetia would not make enough money to pay off the debt to the Russians.

During the next few years, Sutter sent stories to Europe about New Helvetia to be published in French and German. He popularized the idea that he was, as

Previous spread: Fort Ross was constructed in 1812 by Russian-American Company employees who had arrived in 1803 to hunt sea otters and trade the pelts in China and Spanish California. The sea otter population was soon killed off, and the company turned to raising cattle and growing wheat and other crops for the Russian settlements in Alaska.

one German writer called him, Der Koenigin von Sacramento, "the little king of the Sacramento," and encouraged immigrants to settle in the lush California frontier of New Helvetia. Few Europeans came. California was far away, the trip was expensive, and the promise of wealth was quite uncertain. In addition, Sutter set a poor example for prospective immigrant families. Sutter himself had failed to bring his own wife and children from Switzerland.

New Helvetia did attract settlers arriving from the United States, however. In the early 1840s, travel was as primitive as it had been when Sutter began his journey

In the mid-1820s, during an expedition to the Pacific Ocean, William Smyth made a series of sketches of life in California, including one of Mexican cowboys with the Mission San José in the distance. In 1849, Captain B. Schmölder, hoping to attract German and Swiss settlers to New Helvetia, altered the image to show Sutter's Fort in the distance. This later version is shown here.

to California several years before. Some settlers came from the East Coast by sea, others reached Sutter's Fort by wagon or horseback from Oregon. The main route to New Helvetia, however, was the overland trail that led westward from Missouri across the plains, the Rocky Mountains, the Nevada desert, and the mountain passes of the Sierra Nevada. Branching off from the older, better-known Oregon Trail, this California Trail began to bring immigrant parties to California as early as 1841. Before the gold rush of 1849, as many as two hundred travelers arrived each summer.

Sutter welcomed them all. Often he fed them and gave them clothes and blankets. Then he attempted to convince the newcomers to stay near Sutter's Fort, where he offered employment and cheap or free land. He also encouraged another frontier promoter, an American named Lansford W. Hastings, to go to Fort Hall on the Oregon Trail and try to convince Oregon-bound immigrants to turn their wagons toward New Helvetia in northern California.

Always an optimist, Sutter was attempting to build New Helvetia on a foundation of great plans and shaky credit. If he was not already an expert at making promises and inventing excuses, Sutter became one during his first years in northern California.

7. From Mexican to American California

As the 1840s began, John Sutter remained optimistic in the face of his many debts. Especially lucky was the November day in 1841, when twenty-two-year-old John Bidwell arrived at the fort. A former schoolteacher, Bidwell had safely led the first wagon train with women and children from Missouri to California. These were Sutter's long-awaited settlers. Bidwell found Sutter to be welcoming and kind. Sutter in turn recognized that Bidwell was talented and dependable. Sutter hired Bidwell, spent five weeks teaching him Spanish, and then put him in charge of Fort Ross. Next, Sutter gave Bidwell the job of managing Hock Farm on the Feather River, where his young employee supervised the construction of new buildings and generally expanded Sutter's farming operations. The two became lifelong friends, and Bidwell always remained one of Sutter's greatest admirers. Slowly, life at Sutter's Fort was improving.

Juan Bautista de Alvarado, however, was becoming alarmed by the growing numbers of Americans settling in the Sacramento valley. Alvarado's uncle and chief

John Bidwell, shown here in an 1867 photograph by Henry Ulke, was a welcome arrival at Sutter's Fort. He wrote of his first meeting with John Sutter, "Sutter received us with open arms and in a princely fashion, for he was a man of the most polite address and the most courteous manners, a man who could shine in any society."

political rival, wealthy rancher General Mariano Vallejo, and Monterey presidio commander General José Castro shared Alvarado's concern. Vallejo disliked Sutter, who extended his hospitality to new arrivals from the United States, treating them with generosity. However, Vallejo knew that Sutter, as an appointed Mexican official, had the authority to punish Indians, issue passports, and administer justice at New Helvetia, and that Sutter must be dealt with carefully.

Though a leading member of Mexican California's elite, Mariano Vallejo was a champion of democratic government. He believed California should be an independent state governed by a secular, or nonreligious, constitution.

The officials in Mexico City also shared Alvarado's anxiety. Texas had already revolted and broken away from Mexico to become an independent republic. In 1842, the president of Mexico, Antonio López de Santa Anna, sent three hundred soldiers to protect Mexican interests in California under a new governor, Manuel Micheltorena. To protect their own interests, Sutter and Vallejo wanted to gain the new governor's support and friendship.

José Castro commanded the presidio at Monterey, which was built in 1770 to protect Spanish colonial interests from Russian settlement. By 1840, Californios such as Castro had turned their attention to the threat of American conquest.

Micheltorena was likable and friendly, but his soldiers were mostly rowdy ex-convicts who stole chickens, kettles, jewelry, and clothing from California's residents. Sutter made promises to Micheltorena's government and boasted of his success as a settler and an administrator. By 1843, his boasts were proven true. His harvest of wheat and corn had been less than expected, but his fur trappers had caught enough beavers to keep him ahead of his creditors. Though he curried favor with the Californio officials, Sutter's ultimate hope was that the steady arrival of immigrants from the United States would bring settlers, and wealth, to his colony.

This dream appeared to be coming true when, on March 6, 1844, U.S. Army officer Lieutenant John C. Frémont rode into Sutter's Fort with his guide, Kit Carson. The two men explained that their troop of twenty-four men was on a mapping expedition and was suffering from fatigue and hunger. The rest of the

John C. Frémont was a mapmaker and wilderness adventurer who embodied the expansionist philosophy of American politicians such as President James K. Polk. Frémont was responsible for surveying the best-known trails between the Missouri border and the Pacific Ocean.

party would soon be arriving, along with thirty-three starving horses. Sutter's loyalty to the Mexican government was tested. He reported the arrival of an American military force to the Mexican authorities, but he also sent word of Frémont's arrival to Thomas Larkin, U.S. consul in Monterey, exhibiting his increasing loyalty to the Americans. In addition, Sutter showed Frémont his large holdings. When Sutter learned that Micheltorena was sending a force to investigate the arrival of American soldiers, Sutter sent Frémont and his men away from the fort with sixty mules, twenty-five fresh horses, and thirty head of cattle from Sutter's supply. Micheltorena's investigators were met with Sutter's formal welcome, but could gather little information about the Americans. Despite Sutter's generosity, Frémont was cold and even hostile toward Sutter, who he believed posed an obstacle to Frémont's, and America's, plans for California.

After Frémont's departure, politics in California took a confusing turn. Alvarado and Castro led a revolt against Governor Micheltorena. The local Californios did not like the new governor or his ex-convict soldiers. Sutter offered to come to Micheltorena's defense, telling the governor that he had a small garrison of immigrants and Indians who were trained and ready to fight. Micheltorena promised Sutter a second tract of land, known as the Sobrante grant, covering 151 square miles (391.6 sq km), in exchange for military aid. The governor signed the grant papers a short time later in Santa Barbara.

On January 1, 1845, Sutter, who had been appointed a captain in the California militia, marched with his troops, which numbered about 220, from the fort at New Helvetia to the capital at Monterey. When Sutter reached the capital, he was well received by the governor. In the meantime, Castro and the rebels headed south for Los Angeles, where they hoped to rally more support. They convinced local leaders that Micheltorena should be replaced. When the governor marched south with the support of Sutter and some American troops, the southern Californians fought them in a battle at Cahuenga Pass beginning on February 20, 1845.

Numbering about four hundred each, the opposing armies fought for two days. The foreigners on both sides deserted from the battle first, realizing they had nothing to gain by shooting at each other. As a result, Micheltorena's army, originally made up primarily of foreigners, elected to surrender, even though the only casualties were one dead horse and one wounded mule. When the governor agreed to leave the province with his unruly soldiers, California was left in comparative peace. Political control passed to native-born Pio Pico at Los Angeles, and military control passed to José Castro, with headquarters at Monterey.

Sutter surrendered to Castro as soon as the tide of battle turned, though Sutter feared he might be put to death. To Sutter's surprise, Castro received him with kindness, especially when Sutter could prove that he had acted solely on Micheltorena's orders. Sutter returned to New Helvetia without delay, arriving hungry and exhausted on April 1, 1845.

During the spring and summer of 1845, Sutter decided to stay out of Mexican politics, instead focusing on keeping Sutter's Fort financially afloat. He kept a tight rein on the Indians of the surrounding area and tried to put a stop to their cattle rustling. Sutter organized trapping parties and made plans to pay off all of his creditors, especially the Russians, with wheat. His livestock numbered some 4,000 cattle, 1,500 mares, 200 tame horses

Pio Pico, shown here in a photograph from around the 1850s, was dedicated to defending California from outside influences. Of the growing numbers of American settlers he said, "Shall we remain supine, while these daring strangers are overrunning our fertile plains, and gradually outnumbering and displacing us?"

and mules, 3,000 sheep, and assorted hogs, goats, and chickens. His employees were busy manufacturing hats, weaving blankets, distilling brandy, and hammering horseshoes. Sutter had also hired two gunsmiths, two barrel makers, a wagon maker, and several carpenters.

The most skilled carpenter at Sutter's Fort was James Marshall, who had arrived on an overland wagon train in 1845.

Sutter became ever more optimistic about American immigration and saw his land becoming more productive. He still hoped to attract a number of Swiss and German families to his colony. He also expected to welcome some ten thousand Mormons, members of the Church of Jesus Christ of Latter-Day Saints, to California the following summer. The Mormons, fleeing religious persecution in Illinois, were moving west under the leadership of church president Brigham Young. At last all seemed to be going well for Sutter and his plans for an inland empire.

In 1844, President James Knox Polk, who was elected president of the United States on a platform of American expansion in the West, had focused the nation's attention on California. With the support of the U.S. government, John Frémont, previous visitor to Sutter's Fort, left St. Louis, Missouri, in May 1845, on a third expedition to explore the Pacific Coast. He commanded sixty-two soldiers, scouts, and mapmakers, and twelve Delaware Indians. They crossed the Rocky Mountains and the Sierra Nevada, reaching Sutter's Fort in December 1845. They remained as Sutter's guests until mid-January.

Frémont merely indicated to Sutter that he would remain in California through the winter in order to continue mapping. Military commander José Castro gave Frémont permission to map the land if he would stay clear of Mexican settlements. Frémont refused and built an armed camp overlooking the presidio of Monterey. Finally Castro gathered his troops and ordered the American force to leave Mexican territory.

Frémont was heading north up the Sacramento valley on his way out of California when an American marine carrying messages from President Polk overtook him. In response to Polk's correspondence, Frémont returned south to Sutter's Fort, and it was

The flag of California, drawn by William Todd in red paint on a piece of white cotton, was raised in Sonoma on June 14, 1846. The original flag was photographed in 1890, when it was part of the collection of the Society of California Pioneers, but was destroyed in the fires caused by the 1906 San Francisco earthquake. The hand-colored 1890 photograph, shown here, is all that remains.

perhaps no coincidence that he was on hand when a group of Americans calling themselves the Bear Flaggers attacked Sonoma and captured General Mariano Vallejo and his brother Salvador. On June 14, 1846, the American revolutionaries declared California's independence from Mexico, renaming the land the Bear Flag Republic. They took their captives to Sutter's Fort, where Frémont was encamped. Sutter had little choice but to obey the Americans, especially because his future was uncertain under California's new leadership.

The Bear Flag Revolt was little noted outside of northern California and was quickly overshadowed by a larger U.S.-Mexican conflict in Texas, which began in May 1846. The Mexican War began because of boundary issues and the United States's annexation of Texas, but it soon spread across New Mexico and Arizona. The raising of the American flag over Monterey, Yerba Buena, and Sonoma in early July extended the war to California. After six months of skirmishing, the fighting ended on January 13, 1847, at a second battle at Cahuenga. The Americans won the battle, but the conflict continued on several fronts in Mexico during the next year.

Meanwhile, a most unfortunate party of immigrants was making its way across the Sierra Nevada to California. Led by Jacob Donner, a successful businessman with little experience in trailblazing, the party had begun its journey in the spring of 1846, alongside a larger group of frontier settlers. In July, the Donner group parted company with the main party, having decided to take an untried "shortcut" to the barren lands of Utah and Nevada. The torturous route was their undoing. Weeks behind schedule and desperately short of food, the Donner party did not reach the mountains of California until late October 1846. There, they were stopped by the first blizzard of what would prove to be the worst winter in the history of the Sierra Nevada. When a few survivors of an advance party reached Sutter's Fort, Sutter's men made four attempts to reach the stranded and starving travelers, finally rescuing the survivors. Of the 87 men, women, and children in the original party, only 46 remained alive. Sutter fed and cared for all the survivors until they were healthy enough to travel.

The Treaty of Guadalupe Hidalgo, signed on February 2, 1848, ended the Mexican War a year after fighting had stopped in California. This treaty ceded about half of Mexico's territory, including California and much of the Southwest, to the United States. New American arrivals increased California's population during the war. The first large group to arrive was a party of nearly 250 Mormons from New York, led by an energetic convert named Samuel Brannan, who sailed into San Francisco Bay on the ship *Brooklyn* in early July 1846. Later a military force of New York volunteers

also came to Yerba Buena, soon renamed San Francisco, and joined in making this settlement an American trading center.

In July 1847, some four hundred members of the Mormon Battalion, who had marched from Missouri to San Diego to help conquer California, received their army discharge in Los Angeles. Having arrived too late to fight, some Mormons began working in southern California and many traveled north to Sutter's Fort. They intended to head east across the Sierra Nevada to Salt Lake City, the newly established Mormon city near the Great Salt Lake in Utah. However, Brigham Young, president of the Mormon Church, encouraged these men to remain in northern California until the following year. He believed they could earn enough to buy food, tools, seed, cattle, and horses to take to Utah for the support of the church settlement. Sutter hired many of these Mormon veterans to work at his fort. Other Mormons agreed to build a water-powered flour mill on the American River a few miles upstream from the fort.

Two weeks after the battalion veterans started work, Sutter wrote of his good fortune, in his characteristic broken English, to his friend Thomas Larkin at

Previous spread: By the mid–1800s, Americans from all walks of life were building settlements in the far West. Some sought religious freedom, but most came in search of economic opportunities. This map of the United States was created by George Woolworth Colton in 1850.

Monterey: "I have two tannery [workers] and 3 shoe-makers (Mormons) all the hands on my mills are Mormons, and [they are] the best people which ever I has had employed." Sutter went on to compare his new workers with his past employees. "If I would have had Mormons 4 or 5 years past," he told Larkin, "I would have a fortune, but so long I am here I has had only a few good men, the balance was a bad kind of people." Sutter's good fortune, however, would soon take a different turn.

8. Sutter's Gold Rush Failure

John Sutter's future changed dramatically in January 1848. He and his chief carpenter, James Marshall, had formed a partnership to build a water-powered sawmill on the South Fork of the American River at Coloma. Though 40 miles (64.4 km) upstream from Sutter's Fort and well outside the boundaries of Sutter's Mexican land grants, the site was ideal for a mill. It was easy to reach by wagon and had an abundance of yellow pine to supply lumber for New Helvetia. James Marshall set to work building the mill with a crew that included six Mormon Battalion veterans. One of them, Henry William Bigler, was standing close to Marshall when Marshall announced to the work crew assembled at the mill, "Boys, I believe I have found a gold mine."

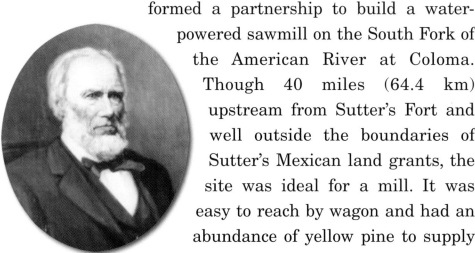

James Marshall later described his discovery, saying, "I reached my hand down and picked it up; it made my heart thump, for I was certain it was gold."

James Marshall stands in front of Sutter's American River sawmill in a daguerreotype taken in 1849. The mill was built in an isolated area known as Cullumah, the Maidu Indian word for "beautiful valley." The name given to the city that grew up around the site after Marshall's discovery, Coloma, is a variation of the Native American word.

In his journal entry for January 24, 1848, Bigler wrote, "This day some kind of mettle was found in the tailrace that looks like gold first discovered by James Martial, the Boss of the Mill." A few days after the first discovery, Marshall went to the fort, taking along more flakes and small nuggets of gold picked up by the Mormon workers. With great secrecy, he showed Sutter the metal. After performing several simple tests, Sutter declared, "It's gold— at least twenty-three-carat gold." A few days later, Sutter visited the sawmill. He walked to the millrace and quickly spotted a few nuggets of gold, which had been planted especially for him to find by Marshall and the Mormon workmen. "By Jove!" the unsuspecting Sutter exclaimed, "It is rich!" Then, as Henry Bigler told the story, Sutter offered everyone a drink from the brandy bottle he always carried in his coat pocket.

Sutter and Marshall tried to keep the discovery secret. They hoped to establish their legal title to the mill property before the public learned that the land was rich in gold. They staked out a land claim, which would give them the right to buy the property when the new U.S. land laws went into effect. They also made a private agreement with Coloma's Indians, who allowed Sutter and his partners to use the land for lumbering and farming for twenty years in exchange for a small annual payment in trade items. Both of these tactics failed. Disputes between federal land commissioners and land claimants delayed land sales in California for years. Meanwhile, Sutter sent a copy of his agreement with the Coloma Indians to Colonel Richard Mason, California's military governor, for approval. Mason rejected the treaty, arguing that private citizens could not make treaties with Indian nations. Only the federal government had that power. Sutter and Marshall were left with no more legal right to the site than anybody else.

Shortly after Marshall's discovery, Bigler and other Mormon Battalion veterans found more gold deposits downstream, away from the sawmill. The most important deposit was located between Coloma and Sutter's Fort, where the South and Middle Forks of the American River came together. There, two of Bigler's friends found gold that was more plentiful and easier to strike than the gold at Coloma. Soon named Mormon Island, the site became the center of the first large-scale placer gold mining in northern California. Placer gold is a phrase to describe flakes that have washed downstream through the course of millions of years. It was abundant in the rivers and streams of the Sierra Nevada's Mother Lode region. Because gold is heavier than the other materials in the riverbed, gravity makes it sink to the base of these deposits, often to the bedrock of the streams. Rather than mining for gold ore deep in rocky mountainsides, California's first miners simply had to sift the gravel and sand in the streambeds and dry streamside beaches and wash the gold free.

In the beginning, California miners used a watertight Indian basket or a metal pan to swirl around the gold and sand mixture, letting the gold settle to the bottom and the water and the lighter sand slosh over the edge. This process is called gold panning. It is easy to learn and requires

Most of Earth's gold is buried under layers of hard rock. In California, however, gold dotted the riverbeds, prompting *New York Tribune* editor Horace Greeley to write, "Fortune lies upon the surface of the earth as plentiful as mud in our streets."

no expensive equipment. As everyone soon discovered, however, it is hard work. The miner must squat or kneel alongside a stream hour after hour, often under a blazing sun, holding a pan in both hands and swirling the water and the sand around and around, hoping to separate out a few gold flakes.

Experienced Mexican miners from Sonora and American miners from placer gold fields in Georgia soon introduced more efficient techniques. They used crudely built mining devices called cradles or rockers that washed the gold-bearing gravels through a slanted wooden tray, with slats across the bottom to collect the heaviest sand and gold flakes, which were then separated by panning. These methods required teams of two, three, or more men to work together. Usually at the end of the week, these teams would trade or sell their gold to a storekeeper or gold dealer, getting fourteen to sixteen dollars an ounce for pure gold, weighed out on delicately balanced scales.

By July, when Governor Mason toured the gold fields, he found two or three hundred people mining at Mormon Island. They were using gold pans, shovels, and rockers to make an average of $100 per day or more. Until this time, the ordinary wage for working men in California had

---

Previous spread: Panning for gold was difficult work, but it held the promise of great wealth and the freedom of the American dream. As one miner wrote to his wife, "Jane, I left you and them boys to procure a little property by the sweat of my brow so that we could have a place of our own—that I might not be a dog for other people any longer."

been just $25 per month. Early in the spring, Samuel Brannan visited Mormon Island and realized the possibilities for making money from the gold seekers. He bought every pan, shovel, and pick axe in the region. He opened a store at Sutter's Fort and stocked it with shovels, picks, flour, coffee, whiskey, and other goods offered at highly inflated prices. On May 12, he returned to San Francisco, stepped off the ferry boat, and walked up a busy city street, holding a bottle of gold dust high in one hand, waving his hat in the other, and shouting "Gold! Gold! Gold from the American River!"

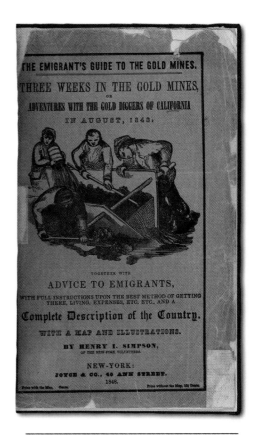

Samuel Brannan's carefully staged announcement, more than any other event, marked the beginning of a worldwide rush to northern California in search of gold. Over the next few years, perhaps five hundred thousand people arrived, coming mainly from North America and South America, Europe, and southern China. It was the largest voluntary

Henry L. Simpson's *Emigrant's Guide to the Gold Mines* was published in 1848. The demand for information about the goldfields of California was great among the hundreds of thousands of young, inexperienced men who would make the journey west.

mass migration the world had ever known. Some eager gold seekers failed, but a great many men and women actually found wealth by either digging for gold, selling goods and services to the miners, running hotels and boardinghouses, or raising farm crops to feed the thousands of people who crowded the mining camps and trading towns throughout the gold country. Sam Brannan was one such success. In the first nine weeks following his San Francisco publicity stunt, he made $36,000.

The gold rush brought both amazing prosperity and new financial dangers to California. Labor and supplies were scarce, and money, mostly in the form of gold dust, was suddenly plentiful. Prices soared. Even successful miners and merchants had to dig deep to pay their living expenses. One Sacramento woman explained the situation to family members back in New York, writing, "Money slips away here about as fast as it is made if one indulges in the common comforts of life; what would last years at home would here disappear in as many months."

John Sutter could not adjust to these changed conditions. His plans for New Helvetia were swept away in the race to the gold fields. He could no longer find laborers willing to work for meager wages when the gold fields promised instant wealth. He could not rule the crowded countryside with his small Indian army or claim title to any piece of open land he desired. He rented out the buildings at Sutter's Fort for $2,000 per month, but he continued to borrow money at high rates of interest to keep up his show of being rich and powerful. By the fall of 1848, he was $80,000 in debt, including what he still owed the Russian-American Company for Fort Ross. His greatest worry was that the Russians would take legal action against him, claiming the New Helvetia grant as payment for his debts. To outwit the Russians, he signed over the title to the land to his eldest son, Johann August Sutter Jr. If he no longer owned the property, Sutter imagined, the Russians would not be able to take it away from

When Johann August Sutter Jr., shown here, arrived at Sutter's Fort in the fall of 1848, he had not seen his father for fourteen years.

him. In a life of missed chances and mismanaged finances, this was Sutter's worst business decision.

Johann August Sutter Jr., commonly called August, had arrived at New Helvetia from Switzerland in September 1848. Only twenty-one years old and inexperienced in business, he was ignorant of American ways and spoke little English. He had not seen his father since he was seven years old, and he scarcely knew what to expect. The elder Sutter appeared to be confused, easily misled, and surrounded by dishonest men. Although August agreed to manage the New Helvetia lands, constant misunderstandings between father and son kept them at odds and their finances in confusion.

Soon after his arrival in California, August formed a partnership with Samuel Brannan and other unscrupulous schemers. These speculators intended to get rich quickly by marketing the New Helvetia lands. Without consulting the elder Sutter, August and his partners had a survey made for the city of Sacramento in an area bordered on two sides by the Sacramento

This 1849 lithograph shows Sacramento's J Street from the riverfront, with the Sierra Nevada in the distance. Soon after the discovery of gold in the American River, Sacramento became a major transportation hub, serving as the western terminus of the Pony Express, the Wells, Fargo & Company shipping route, and the first transcontinental railroad.

and American Rivers and began selling town lots for high, gold rush–era prices. At this point, August became quite ill. Perhaps, as he later claimed, his partners were drugging him. Before he recovered his health, August was cheated of his share of the Sacramento city lands and his partners were suing him for inflated legal fees.

While his son struggled, the elder Sutter moved to Coloma to try his hand at gold mining. His Kanaka and Indian workers cleared $4,000 in gold within a few months. In partnership with Lansford Hastings, Sutter also opened a store at Coloma. The store made money, but Sutter's incredibly bad management and extravagant spending left him still deeper in debt. According to witnesses, during this period Sutter was seldom sober. Early in 1849, he quit mining, sold his share in the sawmill to James Marshall, turned over the store to Hastings, and returned to Sutter's Fort, having somehow failed disastrously while so many others around him prospered.

Business was booming in Sacramento. Countless boats unloaded passengers and cargoes alongside the Sacramento River, and the streets were crowded with merchants and visitors. At Sutter's Fort, however, the only occupations seemed to be drinking and card playing. The fort was filled with gamblers, whiskey sellers, and passing strangers. Sutter's vision of a hardworking rural colony was grower fainter every day. To escape the disorder, August Sutter moved to Hock Farm on Feather River in February 1849. A few months later, his father joined him there. As the elder Sutter later explained, "I had no pleasure to remain there [at Sutter's Fort], and moved to Hock Farm with all my Indians who had been with me from the time they were children." Late in 1849, Sutter sold Sutter's Fort, both the buildings and the land, for a meager $7,000.

August arranged to have Heinrich Lienhard, his father's friend and longtime employee, go to Switzerland and bring back Anna Sutter and the three younger children. August had to borrow part or all of

VIEW OF HOCK FARM, ON FEATHER RIVER, CALIFORNIA.

Hock Farm, which was primarily a cattle ranch, was Sutter's refuge from the squatters who overran Sutter's Fort and New Helvetia following the discovery of gold. The property was located on the Feather River and included a large house, shown in this engraving.

their travel expenses, which totalled $12,000. Anna, daughter Anna Eliza, 20, sons Emil, 18, and Wilhelm Alphonse, 16, and nephew Gustave Schlafi reached San Francisco in January 1850. The Sutter family, especially Anna, had believed they would find "Captain" Sutter living in luxury. On the way to California, Anna had heard impressive stories about her husband. All too soon, she was confronted with the truth.

The Sutter family settled at Hock Farm, where the elder Sutter restrained his drinking and focused on making the farm successful, depending still on his Native American workers. Only on visits to Sacramento or San Francisco, away from his wife and children, did Sutter sometimes share too many bottles of wine or brandy with friends. Tipsy and boastful, John Sutter was quick to recall past triumphs while blaming others for the gold rush disaster he had in fact brought on himself.

9. John Sutter's Final Years

Despite his financial problems, John Sutter tried to maintain a luxurious lifestyle for his family. He sold some surrounding land, raising enough cash to furnish the large home he had built at Hock Farm. He also encouraged August's continued real estate ventures in Sacramento, even though his son had little skill in business. After generously donating sixteen prime lots to the city for public use, August sold many of the remaining parcels for as little as $1 each. Though he managed to sell other parcels for higher prices, he often received no payment. Finally, a desperate August left for Mexico, where he married a Mexican woman. He later returned to California to collect the money that was owed to him, but when he reached Sacramento he sold the rest of his father's property to Sam Brannan and others in exchange for promises to pay. When he had nothing left to sell, August returned to Mexico, leaving his father near to financial ruin. Fortunately, the elder Sutter had signed over ownership of Hock Farm to Anna and continued to farm the area.

Before John Sutter's family arrived, on June 3, 1849, California's new governor, General Bennet Riley, had called a special election for delegates to meet in Monterey in September. They held a constitutional convention to decide between territorial status and statehood, to establish boundaries, and to vote on other issues. Eight delegates, including Sutter, were chosen from the Sacramento district.

This daguerreotype of John Sutter was taken around 1857, by which time Sutter's dream of a western empire was all but destroyed.

Sutter played no major role in the convention proceedings. He took part mainly when an issue affected him personally. The convention delegates honored Sutter by allowing him to be the first to sign the completed constitution and then to deliver the document, together with words of praise from the delegation, to Governor Riley. During the convention, some of Sutter's friends had suggested that he run for governor, but he said that he did not want the office. He later changed his mind, but in the November election, he ran a poor third. Apparently Californians had lost faith in the failed businessman.

California, far exceeding the population of sixty thousand required for statehood, sent its constitution and request for admission to Washington, D.C. The petition created quite a problem in Congress, where the division between northern and southern congressmen over the issue of slavery had reached a crisis. If California became a state, it would not allow slavery, and there would then be sixteen free states and only fifteen slave states represented in Congress. In 1850, Congress approved a compromise that allowed California to enter the Union with the promise that slavery in the new territories acquired from Mexico would be decided by popular sovereignty.

In the Capitol's Senate Chamber, Henry Clay, Daniel Webster, and John C. Calhoun debated the provisions of the Compromise of 1850, which included legislation on slavery, the construction of canals and railroads, and foreign affairs and trade. The Compromise temporarily delayed but did not resolve the tensions that later erupted into civil war.

It also provided that runaway slaves would be returned to their owners. Though the compromise was voted into law, neither side was entirely satisfied with its provisions, and the threat of civil war loomed.

Even though Sutter continued to suffer from financial difficulties, he was still able to enjoy his service in the California militia. He formed a company known as the Sutter Rifles or the Sutter Light Infantry. They hosted a visit from San Francisco's militia company, the Marion Rifles, at Hock Farm on October 28, 1852. The two companies joined in a reception and an evening of formal dancing, with plenty to eat and drink. In February 1853, the California legislature made Sutter a major general in the California militia. He received no salary, but Sutter took pleasure in wearing his uniform, in organizing parades, reviews, and drills, and in planning banquets and conventions. His son Wilhelm Alphonse obtained the rank of colonel of cavalry as an aide to California's governor, John Bigler.

Because California had been admitted to the union as a state, all of the land granted by Spain and Mexico was subject to approval by the U.S. Land Claims Commission. This process was lengthy, difficult, and expensive. Nearly all the original land grant documents were in Spanish, but the U.S. commissioners required that all paperwork be submitted in San Francisco in English. In addition, some of the grants were so large and the boundaries so indefinite that a final decision took several years.

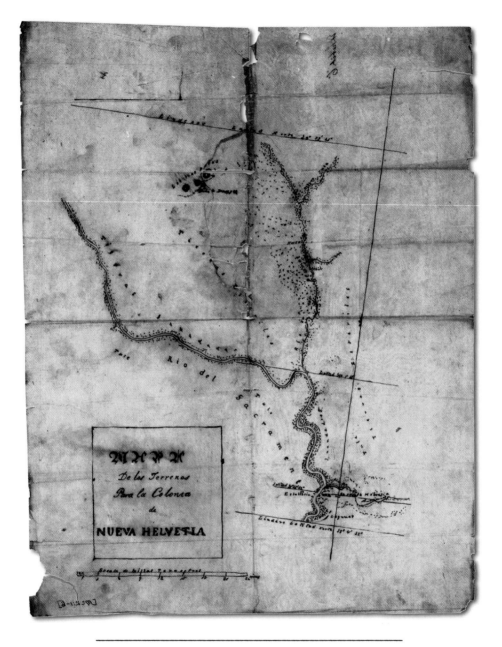

A rough map, labeled "Mapa De Los Terrenos Para la Colonia de Nueva Helvetia," outlines Sutter's original Mexican land grants along the Sacramento and Feather Rivers. It was made in 1851, by John G. Cleal. In the coming years, Sutter's claims to the land would be disputed in the U.S. Supreme Court.

John Sutter sent John Bidwell, his most trusted employee, to San Francisco to defend Sutter's two claims, New Helvetia, his original 75–square mile (194.2–sq km) grant, and the Sobrante grant, nearly 151.6 square miles (392.5 sq km), farther upriver in the Sacramento valley. To Sutter's relief, both grants were approved by the commission on May 15, 1855. As the legal owner of the land, Sutter could sell lots and larger parcels, which he did, to get much-needed cash and to pay off pressing debts. Squatters on Sutter's land, however, appealed the decision to the U.S. District Court for Northern California. Once again, on January 14, 1857, the grants were confirmed. Not giving up, the squatters and their supporters appealed the decision to the U.S. Supreme Court.

In the decision on this final appeal, the New Helvetia grant was upheld, but Sutter's claim to the Sobrante grant was denied. The court said that Governor Micheltorena had officially abandoned the capital at Monterey, and thus lost the right to grant land on behalf of the Mexican government, prior to his signing the Sobrante grant in Santa Barbara. Therefore, the grant was not legal. This decision reduced Sutter's holdings by approximately two-thirds of their original size. Sutter, already in debt, would have to pay back the settlers who had bought parcels of the Sobrante grant during the previous six or seven years. The total amount he owed was overwhelming, but Sutter still had Hock Farm with its orchards and livestock to provide an income.

Sutter managed to make ends meet during the late 1850s and early 1860s with some assistance, in 1862, from the Society of California Pioneers charity. Finally, in April 1864, while the United States was in the midst of civil war, the California state legislature granted Sutter or his heirs a pension of $15,000 per year, payable in monthly installments of $250. This gift was renewed in 1870, 1872, and 1874. Even though the legislature's generosity made it possible for Sutter and his wife to continue living at Hock Farm with a few loyal workers, it did not allow him any extra money.

A final blow to John Sutter's California adventure came when, following his usual custom, the generous Sutter took in a homeless ex-soldier in early June 1865. When he caught the man stealing, Sutter ordered that the man be tied up and whipped. When the man was released, he took revenge. On June 21, 1865, he set fire to Sutter's house, the centerpiece of Hock Farm. The mansion burned to the ground, along with Sutter's clothing, furniture, souvenirs, books, and art collection. John Sutter's optimism finally gave way, and he determined to leave California forever. Five months later, he and Anna sailed for the East Coast, never to return to the land that had caused him so much pleasure and so much grief.

John and Anna Sutter settled in Washington, D.C., where Sutter wrote to his sister-in-law in 1868, "I move in the best society and have to be at the Capitol every day, where I must call upon the senators and members of Congress etc., and you can imagine that I have to be elegantly dressed and that it costs money. . . . I drink no more beer, and wine very sparingly. . . . At 9 o'clock we go to bed, never go to the theatre, and get up again at 5 in the morning, read, and write, etc." Sutter made constant pleas for money from the federal government. He claimed he had been forced into debt trying to pay back the people who had bought New Helvetia land, land that was later restored to Sutter's ownership. With the recent end of the Civil War and the assassination of President Abraham Lincoln, Sutter's claims were not a priority in Washington. He would not relent, however, requesting $50,000 for his losses.

In 1871, finally tired of getting nowhere in the nation's capital, John and Anna Sutter moved to the Moravian town of Lititz, Pennsylvania. Inhabited mostly by German Protestants, the town offered medicinal springs and friendly neighbors. While Sutter faced a bout of rheumatism, or inflamed muscles and joints, his wife oversaw the construction of a sturdy brick house in which they took up residence with three grandchildren, the son and two daughters of August, who was living in Mexico.

Though growing increasingly frail, Sutter made regular trips to Washington, D.C., to press his claims. On June 16, 1880, the U.S. Congress adjourned for the year

On June 20, 1880, the New York Times wrote: *"For years Gen. John Augustus Sutter has been one of the best known of Washington characters. He was a venerable man of large and powerful figure. His head was massive; his face was high-colored and double-chinned. A snowy white mustache and short side whiskers stood in strong contrast upon his flaming complexion. His eyes were keen and dark; his nose was straight and the mouth was firm. He generally wore a dark blue coat with brass buttons, a buff vest, and gray pantaloons. His hat was an old-fashioned yellow plush, broad-brimmed and low-crowned."*

without passing a bill that would have given Sutter $50,000 for his services in the Mexican War. Two days later, on June 18, John Sutter died in his room at the Mades Hotel in Washington, D.C., from what the doctors described as an inflammation of the kidneys. He was seventy-six years old. Annie Bidwell, John Bidwell's wife, happened to be near-by and drove to the hotel to see if she could help in any way. She later wrote to her husband that "General Sutter looked so noble, even in death."

In New York City, the Society of Associated Pioneers of the Territorial Days of California called a special meeting to take action in regard to the death of its president, John A. Sutter. The society's bear

GENL. JOHN A. SUTTER.
BORN FEB. 28TH 1803.
AT KANDERN, BADEN.
DIED JUNE 18TH 1880.
AT WASHINGTON, D.C.
REQUIESCAT IN PACEM

ANNA SUTTER NEE DÜBELD.
BORN SEPT. 15TH 1805.
SWITZERLAND.
DIED JAN. 19TH 1881.
AT LITITZ.

John and Anna Sutter are buried alongside each other
in the Lititz Moravian Church Cemetery, Lititz,
Pennsylvania. This stone marks their grave.

flag hung at half-mast at the hotel, and a memorial service was held before the body was shipped by train to Lititz for burial.

While the body lay in state at the funeral parlor in Lititz, more than five hundred people from the town and surrounding area viewed the body. Sutter was buried in the local cemetery by special permission of the Moravian church. His wife, Anna, died seven months later, on January 19, 1881, and was buried alongside her husband in a common plot. A granite slab giving the dates of birth and death of General John A. Sutter and Anna Sutter marks the grave.

Although Sutter's death did not go unnoticed in California, it was not until August 12, 1939, some one hundred years after Sutter stepped ashore on the south bank of the American River, that ceremonies were held in Sacramento and Lititz to honor the person who might have been California's most controversial pioneer. In 1998, at the 150th anniversary of the 1848 discovery of gold, Sutter's name was again in focus. Praise for his pioneering efforts was tempered by a closer comparison of the Sutter myth and the actual events of his life. A frontier adventurer and promoter with great plans, he was a person who could rightfully boast of many accomplishments, yet one who was all too willing to blame others for his many failures.

10. Understanding John Sutter

Throughout his career, John Sutter depended on his personal charm and skill at self-promotion. In later years, while attempting to get support from the California legislature and the U.S. Congress, Sutter relied on his well-practiced charisma to influence public opinion about his life's work. He began creating his own self-serving version of history. Always ready with excuses, he invented the biggest excuse of all for the disasters brought on by his own bad judgment and irresponsible actions. "Without having discovered the Gold," he wrote in 1856, "I would have become the richest wealthiest man on the Pacific Shore." He continued to make this absurd claim until the very end of his life.

After Sutter had lost his wealth and power and left California, many people were pleased to listen to his story and honor him. He lived long enough to become a historical relic, an amusing old gentleman who gladly repeated the tales about his great service and the great wrongs he had suffered.

Historians, looking at the complete record of his career and personal life, have not been so easily charmed. Hubert Howe Bancroft, California's first major historical writer, visited Sutter in Lititz and heard his lament that he had "been robbed and ruined by lawyers and politicians." "My men," Sutter told Bancroft, "were crushed by the iron heel of civilization; my cattle were driven off by hungry gold-seekers; my fort and mills were deserted and left to decay; my lands were squatted on by overland immigrants; and finally, I was cheated out of all my property. All Sacramento was once mine."

Bancroft summed up Sutter's life in a different way. Sutter, Bancroft declared, "was but an adventurer from the first, entitled to no admiration or sympathy. . . . He came to Cal[ifornia] in the false character of an ex-capt[ain] of the French army. He was great only in his wonderful personal magnetism and power of making friends for a time of all who could be useful to him; good only in the possession of kindly impulses. . . . He never hesitated to assume any obligation for the future without regard to his ability to meet it; he rarely if ever paid a debt when due."

Later historical writers have fastened different labels on Sutter, defining him as a scoundrel, a rascal and an adventurer, a seeker of fool's gold, a ruthless exploiter of Indians, and a failure as a father and family man. Other authors have seen him as a person who

Hubert Howe Bancroft, the son of a midwestern gold seeker, arrived in California in 1852. He settled in San Francisco and opened a successful bookstore. Bancroft soon developed a deep interest in western history, prompting him to collect some 60,000 research documents and to write a 39-volume history of the West. Five of these volumes are dedicated to the history of California, including the western career of John Sutter.

Hubert Howe Bancroft interviewed Sutter at length when preparing his multivolume *History of California*. Bancroft's account showed a well-balanced, critical appreciation of Sutter's role as a frontier speculator who promoted American influence in California while pursuing his own ambitions for wealth and glory.

set in motion large-scale historical changes. One scholar calls him a wilderness entrepreneur. Another historian identifies him as a primary agent in changing the natural world of the Sacramento valley. Sutter, this expert declares, spearheaded the movement to make all nature a commodity for sale. A recent writer is fascinated by the way Sutter's contemporaries celebrated him as though he were a hero. He was really, according to this author, a model for failure.

Despite their different interpretations, these historians agree that it is important not only to understand the events of John Sutter's life but also to see his career as part of a much wider movement in history. From first to last, he was a person made weak, yet famous, by his ambition to achieve great personal fame at any cost. As such, he was a man of his time, a frontier adventurer and promoter who enjoyed his brief years of power and fame, and then proved to be far weaker than he had wished and dreamed and planned and schemed and pretended to be.

Timeline

1803	On February 15, Johann August Suter is born in Kandern, dukedom of Baden.
1826	On October 24, Johann Sutter marries Annette Dübeld. The next day, their son Johann August Sutter Jr. is born.
1834	On May 9, Johann Sutter leaves his family and a heavy debt in Burgdorf.
	On June 12, a warrant for Sutter's arrest is issued. He escapes to France and sails for America. When he arrives in New York, he identifies himself as a captain and former member of the Royal Swiss Guard.
	Sutter travels to St. Louis, Missouri, and enters the Santa Fe trade between Mexico and the United States.
1837	Sutter resides in Westport, Missouri, working as a farmer and an Indian trader.
1838	Sutter leaves Missouri and travels to Fort Vancouver. There he makes plans to travel to California, first sailing to the Hawaiian Islands and then to Sitka, Alaska.
1839	Sutter arrives in Monterey, California, obtains entry papers, and explores the Sacramento and American Rivers.
1840	Sutter is naturalized as a Mexican citizen.
1841	Sutter receives a 75–square mile (194.2–sq km) land grant from Juan Bautista de Alvarado, buys Fort Ross on credit, and begins to build Sutter's Fort at New Helvetia.
1842	Governor Manuel Micheltorena arrives from Mexico.
1844	Lieutenant John Frémont, Kit Carson, and a force of U.S. soldiers arrive at Sutter's Fort.

Sutter is appointed to the rank of captain in the California militia and is awarded a land grant, the Sobrante grant, by Governor Micheltorena.

1845   Sutter aids Micheltorena in combatting a revolt by unhappy military officers and southern Californios.

Micheltorena leaves California.

1846   In May, the Mexican War breaks out in Texas.

The Bear Flag Revolt occurs in Sonoma, and Frémont occupies Sutter's Fort in June. In July, the U.S. Navy arrives in San Francisco.

1847   On January 13, the Treaty of Cahuenga cedes California to the United States.

1848   On January 24, James Marshall discovers gold at Sutter's sawmill.

Johann August Sutter Jr. arrives from Switzerland. The younger Sutter founds Sacramento City in December.

1849   John Sutter Sr. moves to his estate, Hock Farm, on the Feather River and sells Sutter's Fort for $7,000.

Sutter loses the race for governor of California, while gold seekers begin arriving by the thousands.

1850   On January 21, Sutter's wife Anna, daughter Anna Eliza, and sons Emil and Alphonse arrive from Switzerland.

1855   On May 15, the U.S. Land Claims Commission upholds Sutter's New Helvetia and Sobrante grants.

1858   The U.S. Supreme Court denies the validity of Sutter's Sobrante grant.

1864   The California legislature votes to give Sutter $250 per month for 5 years. The pension is later renewed for four more years.

1865	On June 21, an arsonist destroys the Sutter house at Hock Farm.
	Sutter and his family to move to Washington, D.C., where Sutter petitions Congress for money.
1871	Anna and John Sutter Sr. move to Lititz, Pennsylvania.
1879	John Sutter becomes ill with kidney disease and rheumatism.
1880	On June 16, Congress adjourns without approving Sutter's request for financial aid from the government.
	On June 18, Sutter dies at the Mades Hotel in Washington, D.C.

Glossary

apprentice (uh-PREN-tis) An individual who works without pay in order to learn a skill or craft.

bankruptcy (BANK-rup-see) Official declaration by a person or a business of an inability to pay money that is owed, resulting in legal proceedings and loss of property.

caste (KAST) Having to do with levels or groups of people in a society.

confidence man (KON-fih-dents MAN) A thief who lies to and tricks his or her victim.

consul (KON-sul) A very important official sent by his or her government to a foreign country to represent the home country.

debtors' prison (DEH-turz PRIH-zun) An institution where people who owe money to other people are held in punishment.

dowry (DOW-ree) The money or property that a woman brings to her husband when they get married.

entrepreneur (on-truh-pruh-NUR) A businessperson who has started his or her own business.

indelible (in-DEH-leh-bul) Not able to be removed or erased.

indentured servants (in-DEN-churd SER-vints) People who have worked for other people for a fixed amount of time for payment of travel or living costs.

indigo (IN-dih-goh) A blue dye from the indigo plant that was used to color cloth and other items.

millrace (MILL-rays) A fast-moving stream of water that powers a mill wheel.

Moravian (muh-RAY-vee-un) Related to Protestants from Germany who settled in Bethlehem, Pennsylvania, in 1741, and founded missions for Indians in the Ohio valley.

optimistic (op-teh-MIS-tik) Having the most favorable understanding of events or foreseeing the most favorable outcome.

pawnshop (PAWN-shop) A store or business that lends money for goods.

popular sovereignty (PAH-pyuh-lur SAH-vren-tee) Power placed in the hands of the general public to decide an issue.

rendezvous (RON-day-voo) A French word that means an agreed place and time to meet.

rustling (RUH-sul-ing) Stealing cattle.

schooner (SKOO-ner) A fast, sturdy boat with two masts.

squatters (SKWAH-terz) Those who settle on land that belongs to others, and who believe that if they stay there long enough, they will gain the right to the land.

tailrace (TAYL-rays) The device that carries water away from a machine or an industrial site where the water has been used to power or to cool machinery.

tule (TOO-lee) A type of reed that grows in low, swampy places in California.

warrant (WOR-ent) A piece of paper that gives someone the authority to do something.

Pronunciation Guide to the Names of Native Peoples Mentioned in the Text:

Chacumnes	chah-KUM-nays
Maidu	MY-doo
Miwok	MEE-wok
Nez Percé	NEZ PURS
Nisenan	nee-SAH-non
Yalecumne	yah-lih-KUM-nay
Yokuts	YOH-kuts

Additional Resources

To learn more about John Sutter, check out these books and Web sites:

Books

Blodgett, Peter J. *Land of Golden Dreams: California in the Gold Rush Decade, 1848–1858*. San Marino, CA: The Huntington Library, 1999.

Dillon, Richard. *Fool's Gold: The Decline and Fall of Captain John Sutter of California*. Santa Cruz, CA: Western Tanager, 1981.

Hart, James D. *A Companion to California*. Berkeley, California: University of California Press, 1987.

Owens, Kenneth N., ed. *John Sutter and the Wider West*. Lincoln, Nebraska: University of Nebraska Press, 2002.

Web Sites

Due to the changing nature of Internet links, PowerPlus Books has developed an online list of Web sites related to the subject of this book. This site is updated regularly. Please use this link to access the list:

www.powerkidslinks.com/lalt/jsutter/

Bibliography

Blodgett, Peter. *Land of Golden Dreams: California in the Gold Rush Decade, 1848-1858*. San Marino, CA: The Huntington Library, 1999.

Dillon, Richard. *Fool's Gold: The Decline and Fall of Captain John Sutter of California*. New York: Coward-McCann, 1967; reprint, Santa Cruz, CA: Western Tanager, 1981.

Gudde, Erwin G. *Sutter's own story; the life of General John Augustus Sutter and the history of New Helvetia in the Sacramento Valley*. New York, G. P. Putnam's sons, 1936.

Hart, James D. *A Companion to California*. New York: Oxford University Press, 1978.

Lamar, Howard R., ed. *The New Encyclopedia of the American West*. New Haven: Yale University Press, 1998.

Ottley, Allan r., ed. *John A. Sutter's Last Days: The Bidwell Letters*. Sacramento: Sacramento Book Collectors Club, 1986.

Owens, Kenneth N., ed. *John Sutter and a Wider West*. Lincoln: University of Nebraska Press, 1994; Bison Books reprint, 2002.

Owens, Kenneth N., ed. *Riches for All: The California Gold Rush and the World*. Lincoln: University of Nebraska Press, 2002.

Owens, Kenneth N. "Introduction," in *The Wreck of the St. Nikolai*, Kenneth N. Owens, ed. Portland, OR: Oregon Historical Society Press, 1985; reprint, University of Nebraska Press Bison Books, 2000.

Thrapp, Dan L. *Encyclopedia of Frontier Biography*, 3 vols. Glendale, CA: Arthur H. Clark, 1988; reprint, University of Nebraska Press Bison Books, 1988.

Wilbur, Marguerite Eyer. *John Sutter: Rascal and Adventurer; based on source material, manuscripts and letters pertaining to Captain John Augustus Sutter*. New York, Liveright Pub. Corp., 1949.

Index

About the Authors

Iris Engstrand, professor of history at the University of San Diego, received her B.A., M.A., and Ph.D. in history from the University of Southern California. She has taught California history for more than thirty years and is the author of nineteen books on California and the West. These include *San Diego: California's Cornerstone* (1980) and *Quest for Empire: Spanish Settlement in the Southwest* (co-author, 1996). Her numerous articles and book chapters include "John Sutter: A Biographical Examination," in Ken Owens, ed. *John Sutter and a Wider West* (1994). A native Californian, she served on California's Gold-Rush-to-Statehood Sesquicentennial Commission and chairs the Board of Editors for the *Journal of San Diego History*. Dr. Engstrand's academic honors include the University of San Diego's distinguished University Professorship and the Davies Award for Faculty Achievement. She has also received awards of merit from the San Diego and California Historical Societies and the Western History Association.

Ken Owens recently retired as professor of history and ethnic studies at California State University, Sacramento. A graduate of Lewis and Clark College with a Ph.D. in history from the University of Minnesota, he specializes in the study of America's western frontier era. He has written widely on topics concerning the Pacific Northwest and California, including two edited volumes on John Sutter and the California gold rush: *John Sutter and a Wider West* (1994; new ed. 2002) and *Riches for All: The California Gold Rush and the World* (2002). He is the founder of the CSUS Capital Campus Public History graduate program and served on California's Gold-Rush-to-Statehood Sesquicentennial Commission. He became the first faculty member designated for the CSUS Outstanding Teacher Award and has also received the Distinguished Professor Award of the CSUS Alumni Association. He has been honored with the Lifetime Achievement Award from the California Council for the Promotion of History and the Western History Association's Award of Merit.

Primary Sources

Cover (foreground). *John Augustus Sutter*, oil on canvas, circa 1856, William Smith Jewett, from the Oakland Museum of California. **Cover (background)**. Goldminers, photograph, circa 1850, Hulton/Archive by Getty Images. **Page 4**. *John Augustus Sutter*, oil on canvas, 1855, William S. Jewett, held by the State Museum Resource Center, California State Parks. **Page 8**. Map of Germany, from *Kitchin's General Atlas,* printed by Robert Laurie and James Whittle, held in the Map Division of the New York Public Library. **Page 10**. Columbia printing press, 1817, Christel Gerstenberg/CORBIS. **Page 12**. *Artillerie Suisse*, lithograph, 1832, drawn by Maltzheim, engraved and published by Dupuy, held by the Anne S. K. Brown Military Collection of Brown University Library. **Page 15**. *St. Louis from the River Below*, oil on canvas, 1832–33, George Catlin, hedy by the Smithsonian American Art Museum. **Page 16**. Wagon train, engraving, 1839, by Lossing, published in Josiah Gregg's *Commerce of the Prairies: or the Journal of a Santa Fe Trader*, Hulton/Archive by Getty Images. **Page 20**. Fur trader rendezvous, painting, 1837, by Alfred Jacob Miller, held by the Joslyn Art Museum, Omaha, Nebraska. **Page 23**. *King Kamehameha III*, albumen silver print, between 1850 and 1870, by Henry L. Chase, held by the National Portrait Gallery, Smithsonian Institution. **Page 26**. Russian blockhouse, photograph, circa 1900–1930, held by the Prints and Photographs Division of the Library of Congress. **Page 28**. San Francisco, 1884, by Bosqui Eng. & Print. Co., held by the Geography and Map Division of the Library of Congress. **Page 30**. *Juan Bautista Alvarado*, photograph, from the Bancroft Library, University of California at Berkeley. **Page 34**. *Topographical sketch of the gold & quicksilver district of California*, 1848, Edward Otho Cresap Ord, held by the Geography and Map Division of the Library of Congress. **Page 44**. Sutter's Fort, circa 1890–1940, print based on an 1847 engraving by A. Burr, held by the Prints and Photographs Division of the Library of Congress. **Page 47**. *Hock Farm*, oil on canvas, 1851, William Smith Jewett, held by the State Museum Resource Center, California State Parks. **Page 48**. *Map of the gold regions of California*, 1849, James Wyld, held by the Geography and Map Division of the Library of Congress. **Page 50–51**. Fort Ross, by Gideon Jacques Denny, held by the State Museum Resource Center, California State Parks. **Page 53**. New Helvetia, 1849, from *Neuer Praktischer Wegweiser fur Auswanderer Nach Nord-Amerika*, by B. Schmolder. **Page 56**. *John Bidwell*, photograph, 1867, by Henry Ulke, held by the Manuscript Division of the Library of Congress. **Page 57 (top)**. *General Mariano Vallejo*, cabinet card, created by Houseworth & Co., San Francisco, California, held by the Bancroft Library, University of California at Berkeley. **Page 57 (bottom)**. *General José Castro*, photograph, by Arnold of Alameda, California, held by the Bancroft Library, University of California at Berkeley. **Page 58**. *John C. Fremont*, lithograph, circa 1856, by Crehan after Saintin, published by W. Schaus of Boston, held by the Prints and Photographs Division of the Library of Congress. **Page 61**. *Pio Pico*, photograph, circa 1848, held by the Bancroft Library, University of California at Berkeley. **Page 63**. Flag, hand-colored print of the only known photograph of the original, held by the Society of California Pioneers, San Francisco. **Page 66–67**. Map of the United States, 1850, created by George Woolworth Colton and published by J. H. Colton and Co., held by the Geography and Map Division of the Library of Congress. **Page 70**. *James Marshall*, oil on canvas, circa 1914, Alice Brown Chittenden, held by the State Museum Resource Center, California State Parks. **Page 71**. James Marshall at Sutter's Mill, daguerreotype, 1849, by Robert Vance, held by the California Historical Society. **Page 73**. Gold nuggets from California, held by the Oakland Museum of California. **Page 74–75**. Gold-miners, hand-colored daguerreotype, 1850, the collection of Matthew R. Isenburg. **Page 77**. *Three Weeks In the Gold Mines*, 1848, by Henry I. Simpson, published by Joyce and Co., New York, held by the Rare Books & Manuscripts Collection, New York Public Library. **Page 79**. *John A. Sutter Jr.*, photograph, date unknown, held by the State Museum Resource Center, California State Parks. **Page 80**. Sacramento, lithograph, 1849, George Victor Cooper, held by the Geography and Map Division of the Library of Congress. **Page 82**. Hock Farm, engraving, circa 1851, artist unknown, Culver Pictures. **Page 86**. *The United States Senate A.D. 1850*, hand-colored engraving, 1855, Peter F. Rothermel, held by the U. S. Senate Collection. **Page 88**. Sutter's land grants, 1851, copy of the original traced by John G. Cleal, held by the California State Archives. **Page 97**. Hubert Howe Bancroft, photograph, held by the Bancroft Library, University of California at Berkeley. **Page 98**. *The Works of Hubert Howe Bancroft, History of California, Volume XXIII, Vol. VI. 1848–1859*, 1888, published in San Francisco, held by the Bancroft Library, University of California at Berkeley.

Credits

Photo Credits

Cover (portrait) Oakland Museum of California, Oakland Museum of California Kahn Collection; cover (background image), p. 16 © Hulton/Archive by Getty Images; pp. 4, 47, 50–51, 70, 79 courtesy of State Museum Resource Center, California State Parks; p. 8 courtesy of Map Division, The New York Public Library, Astor, Lenox, and Tilden Foundations; p. 10 © Christel Gerstenberg/CORBIS; p. 12 Anne S. K. Brown Military Collection, Brown University Library; p. 15 Smithsonian American Art Museum, Washington DC/Art Resource, NY; p. 20 Joslyn Art Museum, Omaha, Nebraska; p. 23 National Portrait Gallery, Smithsonian Institution/Art Resource, NY; pp. 26, 44, 58 Library of Congress Prints and Photograph Division; pp. 28, 34, 48, 66–67, 80 Library of Congress Geography and Map Division; pp. 30, 57 (top), 57 (bottom), 61, 97, 98 Bancroft Library, University of California at Berkeley; pp. 37, 82, 85 Culver Pictures; p. 53 courtesy of the California History Room, California State Library, Sacramento, California; p. 56 Library of Congress Manuscript Division; p. 63 Society of California Pioneers, San Francisco; p. 71 California Historical Society; FN-30892; p. 73 Collection of Oakland Museum of California; pp. 74–75 Collection of Matthew R. Isenburg; p. 77 courtesy of the Rare Books & Manuscripts Collection, New York Public Library Astor, Lenox, and Tilden, Foundations; p. 86 U.S. Senate Collection; p. 88 California State Archives; p. 93 Maura B. McConnell.

Project Editor
Gillian Houghton

Series Design
Laura Murawski

Layout Design
Corinne L. Jacob

Photo Researcher
Jeffrey Wendt